THE REAL RESURRECTION

THE REAL RESURRECTION

D. H. van Daalen

COLLINS

ST JAMES'S PLACE, LONDON

1972

William Collins Sons & Co Ltd
London · Glasgow · Sydney · Auckland
Toronto · Johannesburg

First published 1972
© D. H. van Daalen 1972
ISBN 0 00 215707 1
Set in Monotype Baskerville
Made and printed in Great Britain by
William Collins Sons & Co Ltd Glasgow

CONTENTS

INTRODUCTION

In recent years there have appeared a considerable number of publications on the resurrection of Christ.[1] That is not surprising. From New Testament times onwards the resurrection of Christ has been presented as the heart of the Christian message. It is therefore inevitable that the present controversies concerning the Church's message should be tied up with the belief in the resurrection and its presentation.

Neither is it surprising that the discussions on the resurrection at times generate a considerable heat. If the resurrection of Christ is the corner-stone of the Christian faith, such discussions cannot but arouse the strongest emotions in those who are genuinely involved in that faith. It is only natural that people should feel strongly about anything that concerns their deepest convictions and that they should resent anything that gnaws at the roots of their faith and seems to undermine the very foundations of their lives. Those who undertake an honest search for truth in a matter of deep Christian concern must expect to arouse strong feelings.[2]

Nevertheless such honest search must be undertaken. Those who have no problems and no questions need not worry. They may be right about what they believe in, or they may be utterly mistaken, but they cannot be expected to concern themselves with questions and problems which they do not see, let alone understand. But those who see certain problems and questions will just have to face them. That is not a matter of unbelief but of integrity. One cannot really believe that God, if one does believe in God at all, looks with special favour on dishonesty and even rewards it.

It is no use saying that the gospel is essentially simple, and that we ourselves create the problems. That may well be very true. It certainly seems that the children and the wise find it easier to believe the gospel. The simple do not see the problems, and the wise can reduce them to size and put them in their proper perspective. But the majority of us are neither simple nor wise. We are somewhere in between, with some education, a little knowledge, a certain amount of cleverness, perhaps also with some sophistication,[3] but rarely with real wisdom. Whether or not that is a good thing is irrelevant: that is what we are, and it would be dishonest not to face the problems and questions which that entails.

The problems and questions concerning the resurrection of Christ naturally fall into three categories. The first deals with the records of the event; the second is concerned with its nature; and the third group concerns the message and the implications of the resurrection. Those three groups are quite different in kind. They therefore require entirely different methods.

Using various methods, according to the matter in hand, a large number of specialists in different spheres have done a tremendous amount of work of extremely high quality in those three fields. But it seems also necessary that the three categories of questions and problems should be brought together under one heading, still varying our methods, but realizing that we are writing about the same risen Lord.

The most important source is the Bible. But a word of warning is necessary. All too often the Bible is used as some special kind of book, a holy scripture, the word of God. That is not the proper use for our purpose.

There is no doubt that those who diligently read the Bible find that God uses this book to speak to us. It is therefore natural that it should assume a certain authority for them, and that they should refer to it as the word of God. That is perfectly legitimate. But the Bible assumes such authority only through its use, by the reader, and, one believes, by God. The authority of the Bible is the outcome of its use, not the hypothesis on which its use is based. Using that authority as a starting-point would be as absurd as proving an argument by its conclusion. That cannot be done in theology any more than in mathematics.

The Bible therefore has to be used, initially at least, in exactly the same manner as any other literature. That does not only mean that we must subject it to the same kind of historical and literary criticism as other books and that the traditions on which parts of it are based have to be examined carefully and critically. It also means that the authors have to be taken seriously as authors. The record of an event does not necessarily prove that the event took place: it only shows what the author thought of the event. And, much more important, what we find presented as God's word is what the author regarded as God's word. Whether or not it was God's word cannot be concluded from the simple observation that the Bible says so.

However, the Old Testament provides evidence of what both Jesus and his early followers regarded as the truth about God; and the New Testament, properly and critically used, provides evidence concerning Jesus Christ and his resurrection. The following pages seek to examine that evidence.

I

THE NARRATIVES OF THE
RESURRECTION

No discussion of the resurrection of Christ can hope to be
fruitful without a careful look at the narratives of the resurrection. No matter how we interpret the resurrection, the
belief in the resurrection of Christ is an undeniable fact of
history. The narratives of the resurrection show us how the
early Christians thought that belief had arisen. Whatever
else they may be, they are evidence of that belief itself and
of the Church's view of its origin.

But they are far more. The Gospels are not eye-witness
accounts taken down immediately after the events. Nor are
they history books in our sense of the word. They were not
written for the sake of an interest in the past. They were
aimed at the present. They are not biographies of a dead
master but they are testimonies to a living Lord. They want
to introduce Christ to the readers.

Actually the word 'readers' is quite misleading. Before the
invention of printing, books were not read silently but aloud,
and 'reading' usually refers to reading aloud to others. Even
the written Gospels are essentially a spoken narrative. Not
only was the Gospel material written down after a long time
of oral tradition but in its written form too, it is a spoken
word, only differing from the oral tradition in that its units
are linked by connecting phrases or passages, and that the
text now has become fixed.

The links between units are editorial. They are essential
to the written book as a composition but they do not reflect
any older tradition. Oral tradition is always concerned with
small units. One can easily check that with one's own mem-

ory of past events. One remembers an incident, where it took place, the main actors involved (but not all of them!), some striking words that were said, but one can rarely remember when it happened, what went before and what came after. The incident is remembered in isolation, and only if it has intrinsic connexions with another event of which the date is known will we be able to place it in time.

But as soon as one wants to write a book relating certain incidents one has to put them in some kind of order and one has to provide some kind of link between them. That is what the Evangelists had to do. And no one should be surprised if they did not all put their material in the same order. Thus, for instance, Mark put all the Jerusalem stories in one block preceding the crucifixion, but John alternates the narrative between Galilee and Jerusalem. The reasons are purely editorial, and have nothing whatsoever to do with the order in which the events happened.

Oral tradition, where it deals with narrative material, is related to the stage rather than the writing-desk. It presents its message in a dramatic form. It is essentially pre-literate, even if it lived in a society where writing and reading were widespread. It is therefore plastic rather than discursive. It does not argue or demonstrate but presents the message in the action. It is therefore quite mistaken to compare it with our Western preaching tradition. Preaching in the West has been greatly influenced by the art of the written word. Many of our sermons are really literary products. One only has to consider how ineffective the average sermon is on television to realize how utterly impossible this type of preaching would have been in the early Church. Nor is oral tradition related to what we know as lectures. Lectures even more than sermons are literary products. They can be heard to advantage only by people used to studying books.

We consequently have to listen to the tradition rather than read it. One therefore cannot expect the Gospels to give the kind of historical information modern historians would like to receive any more than one expects Shakespeare's histories to contain the same kind of information as *The Oxford History of England.*

Oral tradition is geared to a speaker-hearer relationship. It responds to the needs of the community in which it was handed down. It does not develop independently but has a *Sitz im Leben,* a place in the life of the community. It is therefore both creative and selective.

Its creativity however is not random fantasy, nor is it the individualistic creativity of the post-Renaissance artist. Sayings and stories which arise in oral tradition are usually *ben trovato,* they not only answer the situation in which they arose but often characterize the person to whom they refer better and more concisely than actual 'historical' sayings and events. A good example from the later history of the Church is Luther's famous declaration, 'Here I stand, I can do no other'. He may not actually have spoken those words, yet it would be difficult to sum up the man and the situation more concisely.

In the early Church one important factor was added to this. To the early Church the belief in the resurrection of Christ and the work of the Holy Spirit was no mere theory. The risen Lord was a living reality. He would therefore be in a position to interpret and add to the words which he had spoken when in the flesh (though he would naturally not be expected to contradict them).

But the tradition is also selective. Stories and sayings were not handed down simply because they were there but because they met a definite need and had a definite function to fulfil.

All that we have said holds good even if it could be proved that Mark had his information directly from Peter and that the Beloved Disciple was the apostle John. Even if a story is told by the same person, often enough it develops. We have all met the old sailor who won the Battle of Jutland single-handed. There is no evidence that the early Church had a surfeit of such persons. There is a dead-pan straightforwardness in the New Testament accounts that speaks of the reliability of the witnesses. Even so, an event of the past can take on a new significance. One may remember points which one never noticed at the time. Above all, if the story is a means of communication, one must tell it in such a way that the message gets across. The professional historian aims at a reconstruction and reproduction of the past. But the story-teller, and particularly the Evangelist, wants to communicate a message. A small incident in a theatre in Paris during the First World War may illustrate the point. A play had been running for a considerable time, in which a father received the message that his only son had died. The actor concerned had always played the part with considerable noise and lamentation and made a profound impression on the audience. But one night he just stood, without saying a word. After the performance, when challenged by the producer, he said, 'I learned this morning that my son died at the front'. One can understand the actor, but he was mistaken. For as an actor his job was not to reproduce the father's grief but to communicate it to the audience. And that requires more than photographic accuracy. Similarly those who demand photographic accuracy from the New Testament are asking for the wrong thing altogether. Accuracy must sometimes be sacrificed in the cause of communicating the truth.

Nevertheless we should not forget that the time for the tradition to develop was relatively short. By the time the Gospels were written there were still people alive who had known the Jesus of history. Their memory of particular events would not always be accurate, and in any case people were not interested in any photographic accuracy. But it was still known what kind of a man Jesus was. And the events remembered, though not always with accuracy, would still be real events. It would be foolish to doubt that the tradition has real substance and deals with real events concerning a real person.

I. MARK'S NARRATIVE

The Gospel according to Mark contains two stories relating to our subject, Mark 15: 42-47 and 16: 1-8. The first is that of the burial of Jesus. The Evangelist tells us how a man from Arimathea, called Joseph, asked for permission to bury the body of Jesus, received such permission, buried the body in a tomb in the rock, rolled a stone in front of the grave, and how two women, Mary Magdalene and Mary the mother of Joses, watched him do that.

But who was Joseph? Mark says that he was a member of the council but does not tell us which council. Luke takes it for granted that it was the Sanhedrin (Luke 23: 51). That seems likely, though there may have been a city council like there were in some other cities of the Roman Empire, and he could have been a member of that. Mark further refers to him as 'excellent'. That may refer to character, position or wealth. Luke elaborates on the first, Matthew on the last interpretation (Matthew 27: 57), while most modern translators prefer the second (Revised Standard Version, New English Bible: 'respected'; Jerusalem Bible: 'prominent'). More important is the question what is meant by 'looking for the kingdom of God'. Matthew interprets it as meaning that he was a disciple in the wider sense of the word, not one of the band of followers but someone who had heard Jesus' teaching. But do Mark's words allow of that interpretation? E. P. Gould and Ernst Lohmeyer think not,[1] and it is indeed difficult to see why, if Mark wanted to convey that Joseph was a disciple, he did not say so. It is easy to see how later Christians, to whom the kingdom of God was identical with the Gospel, would arrive at that conclusion, but that does not mean that it is correct. Moreover, the women who watched the burial evidently did not know him. Of course, it is quite likely that not all those who had heard the teaching of Jesus knew each other well. But Mark seems to suggest, not only that Joseph was a total stranger but that the women had reason to be afraid. And surely, had Joseph been a follower of Jesus, the natural thing for him would have been to contact some of his closer disciples. It seems reasonable to assume that Mark means exactly what he says and no more: that Jesus was buried by an outsider, an excellent man of some importance, and one who shared the messianic hopes either of the Pharisees, or of the more apocalyptic circles, and who was perhaps, but not certainly, also a member of the Sanhedrin. Lohmeyer suggests that the earliest tradition spoke only of a nameless pious Jew.[2] If so, Mark or his source has done no more than give him a name, for he shows no knowledge of the later Joseph legend. But the man who buried Jesus must have had a name, and there is no reason why this name could not have been Joseph, not after all such an uncommon name.

But what was Mark's purpose in telling the story? The reference to the women (15: 47) is obviously connected with the identification of the grave. But also the fact that Jesus was buried by an outsider may have been more significant to Mark than it may appear at first. The rumour that the disciples had stolen the body was circulated at an early date. The suggestion that the owner of the grave might have had a hand in this must have seemed obvious. The tradition that he was not connected with the band of the Lord's disciples may not have been invented to contradict this, but it would still have been a useful argument. We cannot be certain that this was in Mark's mind, but it does not seem unlikely.

The other Marcan story is about three women visiting the grave early on Sunday morning. Mary Magdalene is one of the two mentioned before as having seen the burial. They had bought spices when the sabbath was over (Mark 16: 1), that is to say, on Saturday after sundown, evidently to perform some final acts of piety which had been left undone on the Friday. There is no suggestion in Mark that the arrangements on the Friday had been incomplete, and we do not know that it was the custom to anoint the dead; but there is nothing unnatural in the desire to do some last thing for the dead, however superfluous. The women wonder what to do about the stone used as a door to the tomb, but when they arrive they find that the stone has been moved, and as they go in they meet a young man in white, presumably regarded by Mark as an angel, who tells them that Jesus the Crucified is risen, that he is not here, and that they must go and tell the disciples and Peter that he is going before them to Galilee, where they will see him. The women flee in terror, and tell nobody. That must, of course, not be taken too literally. Mark means that the story was not told outside their immediate circle.

It is important to note that what the women observe is not the absence of the body but the presence of the messenger. Also that he does not say, 'Look, the body is not here, therefore you can see that he is risen', but, 'He has risen, (therefore) he is not here'. The women are invited to look into the tomb, but we are not told whether or not they did. We are, in fact, not even told that the tomb was empty, only that Jesus was not there. It does seem that the emptiness of the tomb is implied, but it is not stated, and it is not regarded as evidence of the resurrection. However, the resurrection of Christ makes any attention to the tomb superfluous.[3]

It has been suggested that the story of the open tomb may be an attempt to stop any cult of the Lord's grave.[4] However, we have no evidence of such a cult. If it does not relate an actual historical event, it seems much more likely that the story grew naturally out of the belief in the resurrection: to first-century Jews the empty tomb would be an almost inevitable conclusion from the belief that the Lord was risen. All the same we must not forget that when the Gospel was written some of the witnesses had died only recently and that the tradition itself must date back to a time when the majority were still alive. We should also note that we have no evidence that even opponents of the Christian faith questioned the fact that the tomb was empty. It seems therefore that the arguments against the story of the empty tomb are by no means so formidable as is sometimes suggested.

But so much is certain, that the empty tomb is not, and never was, proof of the resurrection, and that the proper worship of the Lord is not at his grave but in the midst of his people: 'He has risen, he is not here' (whatever may or may not be in the tomb).

Was it Mark's intention to end his Gospel here? The arguments against 'for they were afraid' being the end of the Gospel are formidable. In the Greek text, 'for' is the end of the sentence, and of the book. 'For' as the end of a sentence is not unique.[5] But it would be unique as the end of a book. Moreover, is it likely that Mark should end his Gospel without so much as one appearance of the risen Lord, that is without any story of the resurrection proper?[6] Is it possible for Mark to have written his book without relating how the disciples came to believe in the risen Lord?[7] That after all is what the Gospel is about!

Attempts have not been lacking to complete the Gospel. Mark 16: 9-20 is an early attempt at this (the same cannot be said of the 'shorter ending' of some manuscripts, as this concludes the Gospel only in a formal manner[8]). In recent years it has been suggested that parts of Mark's lost ending can be found in Mark 6: 45-52; 8: 27-30 and 9: 2-13. But even if one or more of those passages reflect post-resurrection experiences, this is no evidence that they were ever part of the lost ending of Mark and have been transposed at some later date. There is no evidence that Mark regarded them as other than stories relating to the Lord's earthly life.

There is, in fact, no evidence that the Gospel did not end with 16: 8. Not only do the best manuscripts end there but it is obvious that both Luke and Matthew used copies of Mark's Gospel which did not go beyond verse 8. Lohmeyer, in his commentary on Mark, brings together a number of arguments why this verse must be the end of the Gospel as intended by Mark.[9] We shall not repeat those. But one additional argument must be mentioned because it seems

conclusive. The opening words of the Gospel, 'The beginning of the gospel of Jesus Christ, the Son of God', are
usually interpreted, 'Here begins the gospel . . .' But is this
really what the phrase means? Is it not much more likely
that this is the title of the book? If the gospel can be adequately summarized as 'Christ and the resurrection', or even
only 'the resurrection', then the content of Mark's book,
leading up to but not including the resurrection, is precisely
The Beginning of the Gospel of Jesus Christ, the Son of God. The
continuation, the gospel proper, is the life of the risen Lord
with his people. The appearances of the risen Lord belong to
this gospel proper. They do not belong to his earthly life,
not to the beginning of the gospel but to his new life.

There is, however, another reason why the appearances
are not mentioned and probably not even hinted at. To
Mark the resurrection of the dead is an eschatological event,
indeed *the* eschatological event:[10] it is the end of human
history. He knew that history had not ceased on the day of
the resurrection of Christ. And he can scarcely have been
unaware of the Lord's appearances. Yet he does not only
refrain from describing them but probably does not refer to
them at all. Lohmeyer's argument that the reference to
Galilee in verse 7 points to the Parousia, not to the appearances, may not be conclusive but it certainly is plausible.[11]

There is a tension between the belief that the resurrection
of Christ is the eschatological event, and the fact that
history has carried on as before. Mark has avoided the
difficulties arising from this by ending his Gospel where he
did. We are not suggesting that he did that deliberately in
order to avoid those difficulties. It seems unlikely in the
extreme that he was even consciously aware of them. It is
much more likely that he was guided by a good writer's
instinct. But at any rate he has avoided the trap into which
others have fallen.

2. MATTHEW'S NARRATIVE

Matthew's story of the burial is clearly dependent on Mark. It contains nothing that the author could not have concluded from what he found in the earlier Gospel. The only apparently fresh information, that Joseph was a disciple of Jesus (Matthew 27: 57), is, in fact, Matthew's interpretation of 'looking for the kingdom of God' (Mark 15: 43).

The story of the guard at the tomb is new (Matthew 27: 62-66). It is also found in Pseudo-Peter (fragments 28-49), in a more elaborate and clearly later form. But is it a reliable, or even an early tradition?

Some of the objections raised against the story do not really hold water. It has been said that according to Mark the women on the Sunday morning intended to go into the tomb (Mark 16: 1-4), which they would not have contemplated had they known there was a guard. Quite so. But if there had been a guard, could they have known?

The argument for the story is much stronger than may appear at first. Once it is conceded that the Gospels contain accurate information as to what happened at the trial of Jesus, it seems reasonable, indeed almost inevitable, that the authorities should take some steps to prevent any rumours being spread about the 'third day' (Mark 14: 58; Matthew 26: 61).[1] But it must be doubted if the New Testament contains this kind of accurate and detailed historical information. It seems much more likely that the story should have arisen from first-century controversies about the empty tomb.[2]

In a controversy of this kind, in which the Christian community was accused of having staged the resurrection by removing the body, it was almost inevitable that sooner or later somebody would object, 'But surely the authorities would not have left the tomb unguarded'. Once the suggestion was made it was almost bound to develop into the kind of story we find in Matthew.

But whether or not the story of the guard is historical, it

points to a controversy in which both parties agreed that the tomb was empty. How it came to be empty, that was the question.

The story of the empty tomb (Matthew 28: 1-7) is dependent on Mark. The names of the women are harmonized with Matthew 27: 61 =Mark 15: 47, the young man is identified as an angel, and we are told what Matthew thought this angel's job was: to let the women look into the tomb. Thus it is he who moves the stone, not to let Jesus out but to let them in. His words are paraphrased. The awkward 'and Peter' is omitted, and the final words are adapted to Matthew's understanding of the reference to Galilee. He knew of no tradition that Jesus had foretold that he would appear there after his resurrection; and it must be doubted if he knew of any to the effect that Jesus had actually appeared there. But he was convinced that the messenger's words referred to such an appearance, not to the Parousia,[3] and paraphrased accordingly.

The Christophany in verses 8-10 seems to repeat the angelophany of verses 2-7. It is possible that in one stream of the tradition the young man was identified not as an angel but as the risen Lord himself, and that Matthew, not realizing that he was dealing with two versions of the same story, put them both in. But we cannot be certain that this is not another story.

The following verses (11-15) round off the story of the guard, and Matthew ends his book with one appearance in Galilee.

The scene on the mountain (verses 16-20) gives a summary of the Lord's post-resurrection teaching, coloured by the Church's teaching of Matthew's own days.[4] The 'mountain to which Jesus had directed them' seems rather vague, and the Lord's words seem rather general. That makes one wonder if these verses are really based on tradition or whether the whole scene is based on the Evangelist's understanding of Mark 16: 7. The latter seems very likely[5] but one cannot be certain.

3. LUKE'S NARRATIVE

Like Matthew's, Luke's narrative of the burial (23: 50-55) contains nothing that the author could not have concluded from what he found in Mark. He takes the council to be the Sanhedrin and takes it for granted that Joseph could not have consented to their purpose and deed. He does not identify the women, but adds that 'on the sabbath they rested according to the commandment', which was implied in Mark.

The story of the women at the tomb differs from Mark's on five or six points. Where Mark has one man (Mark 16: 5), Luke has two (Luke 24: 1-11). The identical phrase, 'behold, two men', is found in the story of the transfiguration (Luke 9: 30, but not Mark 9: 3) and in that of the ascension (Acts 1: 10). Is this an attempt to link the three events[1] and are the two men Moses and Elijah (as in 9: 30)? Or have the two men come from a tradition similar to that underlying John 20: 11-18? Or is it just that Luke likes to have two witnesses of important events, as, for example, Simeon and Anna being witnesses at the presentation in the Temple (2: 25-28), Herod and Pilate both witnessing to the innocence of Jesus (23:1-25), and two men meeting the risen Lord on the way to Emmaus (24: 13-32)?

Secondly, the women actually enter the tomb and see that the body is not there. It seems reasonable to interpret Mark as inferring that, but Mark does not really say more than that the women, as they enter, see the young man.

Thirdly, Mark's reference to the disciples seeing the risen Lord in Galilee has now become a reference to his teaching in Galilee. Unlike Matthew, Luke was firmly convinced that no appearances took place there, and he seems to have changed the words accordingly (24: 6-7).

Fourthly, Luke informs us that the women told the disciples about their experience, while Mark states that they said nothing to anybody (Mark 16: 8; Luke 24: 9). This difference, however, is only apparent. Mark only wanted to convey that the story was not made public.

In the fifth place there is a discrepancy about the names of the women.

And finally, if verse 12 is authentic, Luke has added a visit by Peter to the tomb. New Testament critical scholarship generally has regarded it as spurious. Westcott and Hort regarded it as a 'Western non-interpolation', the Nestle text omits it, and so do a number of modern translations (for example the Revised Standard Version and the New English Bible); but Moffatt and the Jerusalem Bible retain it. A. R. C. Leaney has recently argued for the genuineness of the verse.[2] The manuscript evidence is certainly overwhelmingly in favour of its retention. Of Greek manuscripts only D (codex Bezae) omits it; it is further omitted by some important Old Latin and Syriac manuscripts, and is absent from Marcion's text. Saying therefore that 'other ancient authorities' (Revised Standard Version) or 'some witnesses' (New English Bible) add verse 12, is a vast understatement: all Greek manuscripts do except one, and it would be rash to take it for granted that the verse must be spurious.

If, however, verse 12 is genuine, then it is not only obvious that it comes from a source other than Mark (unless Mark did not end with 16: 8), but one must also ask if Luke followed only Mark in the preceding verses. It seems likely that verse 12, if it was not added afterwards from John 20: 3-10, has come from a tradition very much like that used by John. Luke's omission of the Beloved Disciple need not mean much: as is shown by the Acts, and perhaps also by Luke 5: 1-11, he attaches great importance to the unique significance of Peter, and Luke 24: 24 shows that Luke too knew that more than one disciple had visited the grave. There is also evidence in other parts of both Gospels that Luke and John had access to similar traditions,[3] though it must be doubted if they used a common written source.

The question is, is there any indication in the verses 1-11 that Luke used, for these particular verses, any source other than Mark, and, if so, was that source similar to John's? There is little evidence that he did. The only point that could be regarded as such an indication is the presence of two men, not one. It seems just possible that Luke may have had some additional information besides what he found in Mark. But if he had it still does not add anything significant to Mark's story of the women at the grave. The only really new information in verses 1-11 is that the disciples did not believe the women. But that he could conclude, though not from Mark, from the ensuing events: it is governed by verses 13-27. Verse 11 does, however, tell us something about Luke's appreciation of the story of the open tomb. Whatever its significance – and there is no doubt that to Luke the story was significant – he certainly did not regard it as the ground of the belief in the resurrection. Such belief comes from *meeting* the risen Lord, not from seeing an empty grave. Verse 12, if genuine, confirms this: Peter wonders.

The remainder of the Gospel tells us how some of the disciples did meet the Lord. With consummate skill Luke puts that within the compass of one night. Luke is not a chronicler but an artist, who does not want to diffuse his material. Especially in the Acts of the Apostles, where he could work with greater liberty than in the Gospel, he shows his skill in arranging his material, and often condenses the events of a long period into one impressive scene,[4] thus bringing out the true significance of the events. Here too that method is used to great effect.

He first tells the story of the Lord's appearance to two men on the way to Emmaus (24: 13-32). Though we are well aware of Luke's ability to write a convincing story without much material, there is little reason to doubt that he used traditional material. The story contains some striking and interesting points. The first is the ordinariness of the Lord's appearance. Admittedly the men did not recognize him, which Luke explains by saying that 'their eyes were kept from recognizing him', but which would be entirely natural: one does not expect someone who has died to walk beside one.[5] But it never occurs to the two men that there is anything 'supernatural' about their companion, and they never suspect that he might be other than just a stranger staying at Jerusalem until he breaks the bread, gives it to them and disappears from their sight. There was nothing of the 'disembodied spirit' about the appearance of the risen Lord.

Secondly, the words of the risen Lord do not contain any esoteric teaching but are confined to an interpretation of the Scriptures. It has been remarked that the Old Testament does not contain any detailed prediction of Christ's passion and resurrection.[6] But the story does not contain any of those exercises in artificial exegesis to find such detailed predictions, which were so popular in the early Church. In this passage it is rather the whole of God's dealings with his people Israel that has been fulfilled in the passion and resurrection of Christ. No artificial exegesis is needed to show that, and the Evangelist refers to the Old Testament as a whole, not to a number of proof texts. That is particularly interesting as the New Testament already shows quite a number of advanced specimens of forced exegesis to show that the Old Testament predicted in detail what happened to Jesus. It is true that Luke's readers did not need proof texts to the same extent as some other New Testament readers. But would Luke have removed the proof texts, had he found them in his material?

Thirdly, the recognition of the Lord came in the breaking of the bread. There can be no doubt that Luke and his readers would immediately think of the Eucharist, in which they themselves met their living Lord.

The verses 33-35 are a link between two parts of the narrative. They are obviously editorial, and really a little awkward. How could the two men expect to find anybody waiting for them at that time of the night? But, of course, one should not ask such questions. These verses only serve the aims of composition: they link two traditional stories and keep the action within the framework of one day. Nevertheless they contain the interesting information that the Lord had appeared to Peter. Paul too knew that Peter had been the first to see the risen Lord (1 Corinthians 15: 5). We shall see that the story of the appearance at the lakeside (John 21), in which Peter plays such a prominent part, has the character of a first appearance. The story was known to Luke in another form (Luke 5: 4-11). There is no telling whether Luke received it as a story from the early days of the Lord's ministry, or whether he received it as a post-resurrection story and, convinced that no appearances took place in Galilee, transferred it to the earlier ministry. As it is, Luke refers to the appearance to Peter only in the short notice in 24: 34.[7]

The final story is one of an appearance to the Eleven. Luke goes to great length to show that the Lord has risen with an ordinary body. As the story stands that is one, though not the only, purpose of the eating of the fish. But two points should not be overlooked. One is that, in the early Church, fish was connected with the Eucharist. The other is that, to Jewish people of that time, 'spirits' would be those who are in Sheol or Hades. The characteristic thing about those in Sheol is not that they are disembodied but that they are *dead*. The Lord's reply, 'See my hands and my feet, that it is I myself; handle me, and see . . .', wants to establish first and foremost, *who* it is that has appeared to them, and that he is *alive*. Luke's massive interpretation of the resurrection ('for a spirit has not flesh and bones . . .') should not make us forget that even in Luke's narrative the emphasis is on the recognition of the risen Lord, not on what has appeared but on who has appeared.

The Lord's words carry on the teaching of the earlier story. It should be noted that the word translated 'fulfil' does not normally mean 'come true'. It normally means, 'make full', 'fill up', usually in the sense of 'satisfy'. Here too Luke's source seems to take us back to before the 'proof text' stage.

The Eleven are now given definite instruction to preach and are promised power from on high. To Luke the Holy

Spirit is the power of God made available to the believers.

The Gospel ends with Jesus' farewell and the disciples' return to the city. The reference to the 'ascension' is a later gloss. The story is not meant to be an account of the ascension but a summing up of the Lord's post-resurrection teaching.

4. THE NARRATIVE OF THE ACTS

The picture Luke gives us in the Acts of the Apostles differs considerably from that in his Gospel. That is not due to his having received additional information[1] but simply to the different purpose and scheme of the book.[2] In the Gospel he wants to give a vivid picture of the resurrection of Christ, and he achieves that by presenting, after a short preliminary story about the empty tomb, one dramatic and impressive account of two appearances of the Lord. But the Acts describe the continued life of the risen Christ with his people. Thus the continuum of time becomes important, and some reference has to be made to the 'forty days'.

At the same time he uses the opportunity to answer some awkward questions. Why, if the great eschatological event has taken place in the resurrection of Christ, has not the Kingdom come? Luke does not know: God may know, and, of course, he does know. It is good to put on record that Christ himself has said something to that effect (Acts 1: 7). Mark has the answer in another context and form (Mark 13: 32).

In the farewell scene (the 'ascension', Acts 1: 6-9) many commentators (and artists!) have overlooked that clouds do not normally shoot up and down but appear to move more or less horizontally. It is naïve to assume that the ancients had not observed that as well as we do. The cloud is therefore not a vehicle to carry Jesus upwards.[3] Throughout the Old Testament clouds are symbolic of the glory of God (for example, Exodus 16: 10; Leviticus 16: 2; Numbers 9: 15-22; Deuteronomy 1: 33; 1 Kings 8: 10-11; Psalm 78:

14; Ezekiel 1; Daniel 8), as, indeed, they are in the New
Testament (Luke 9: 35).[4] That is also the function of the
cloud in this passage. That does not mean that Luke did not
regard the ascension as a physically observable event. The
Christian Church did not arise in a vacuum.[5] The early
Christians expressed their experiences in the language of
their days. They thought like their contemporaries, they
shared their understanding of the world, and they actually
saw things accordingly. It would be absurd to expect Luke
to have described the event in our terms. But it would be
equally absurd to overlook that to him the lifting up, the
cloud and heaven were more than a movement, an object
and a place: Jesus is now raised (lifted up) to the glory of
God (the cloud) and exists in the manner of God (heaven).

The words of the two men (angels? or Moses and Elijah?)
refer once more to the awkward question of the 'postponed'
Parousia. The life, death and resurrection of Christ, his
ascension, the story of the Church, and finally the Parousia
are all placed in one historic connexion. But by trying to
historicize the resurrection and the Parousia Luke has given
them a mythological form.

The opening verses of the Acts refer to the earthly life of
Jesus as 'all that Jesus began to do and teach'. That reminds one of Mark 1: 1. The inference is that the Acts of the
Apostles deals with what Jesus continued to do after his
ascension. The whole of the book can be regarded as a post-
resurrection narrative about Jesus.

Between the Lord's earthly life and his post-ascension
work there were the forty days of the appearances. Luke is the
only New Testament writer to refer to any such specific time.
After the forty days there are no more appearances. Luke
does record the appearance to Paul on the road to Damascus
but regards that as being in an entirely different category.
The ascension is the end of the time of God's revelation and
the beginning of the time of the Church. Nevertheless the
Lord is not absent. Through the Holy Spirit he continues to
be with his people and to work in the world.

5. JOHN'S NARRATIVE

Right from the beginning John goes his own way, independent of Mark. The differences are very considerable. Mark knows nothing of the request of the Jews that the bodies should be removed (John 19: 31-37). Neither does he tell us that the tomb was in a garden close to the place of the crucifixion (though that may have been implied) and that it was a new grave. John does not tell us that the grave was closed with a stone (though 20: 1 obviously infers this), nor does he mention the women watching the burial. He is the only one to mention Nicodemus. In fact the only common factor in the story is Joseph of Arimathea, who is here a disciple of Jesus who has kept his discipleship a secret (something he has in common with Nicodemus). The burial is an elaborate one and the story in no way prepares for the next scene.[1]

The story of the Easter morning (20: 1-18) offers considerable difficulties. Bultmann notes[2] that there seems to be some competition between two stories, one of Mary Magdalene at the tomb, and one of the two disciples, and comes to the conclusion that the combination cannot be original. The real problem is not that Mary first leaves the tomb and then we find her back without being told that she returned. Surely her return is implied. But it seems strange that the two disciples should just leave her without telling her of their experiences.

The question however is, what does and what does not belong together? Was the story of the two disciples inserted in the story of Mary Magdalene?[3] Or are verses 1-10 one story and 11-18 another? And if the latter is the case, does Luke (24: 22-23) have the original story, without any connexion with Mary Magdalene? But how is it then that Mary Magdalene figures both in the Synoptic and the Johannine version of the empty tomb?

In the story as it now stands, Mary's first visit to the tomb differs from Mark's story in that she is alone, and that she sees no one. She arrives at the logical conclusion that someone must have removed the body.

The story of the two disciples is very graphic. The details about the linen cloths and the napkin serve to show that the body had not been stolen: which tomb-robber would have bothered to undress the body first and fold the cloths? But what is the significance of the end of verse 8, 'and believed'? It is generally assumed that the author wants to distinguish between the Beloved Disciple who did, and Peter who did not believe.[4] Actually we are not told whether Peter did or did not, and Bultmann suggests that the author means that Peter believed and that the phrase just states that the other disciple also believed.[5]

And what did they believe? It is tempting to paraphrase, 'believed that the body was gone'. After all it would be unique if anybody had come to the full Christian faith in the risen Christ merely by seeing an empty tomb. That would certainly be at variance with everything we find elsewhere in the New Testament. But when the Gospel according to John uses the word 'believe' without mentioning the object, it is invariably referring to faith in the full Christian sense of the word.[6] Spitta regards verse 8b as a gloss.[7] This seems a daring conjecture, without any manuscript support, but would make much better sense of verse 9. The whole story then becomes another example of how the empty grave posed questions and did not lead to faith. Apparently the version quoted in Luke 24: 22-23 made the same point.

The remaining part of the story shows us Mary Magdalene at the tomb. She sees two angels to whom she repeats her complaint that 'they have taken away my Lord' but who do not attempt to make her any the wiser. This is done by Jesus himself, whom at first she does not recognize. Here too we are struck by the ordinariness of the appearance, the same as in Luke 24: 13-32: she thinks he is the gardener. Only when he speaks her name does she recognize him. The final words of the scene at first sight seem rather baffling. She is told to let go of Jesus 'for I have not yet ascended to the Father; but go to my brethren and say to them, I am ascending to my Father and your Father, to my God and your God'. Does he mean that when he has ascended to the Father, everything will be as it was before, and she will be able to touch him? Surely we must not press the word 'for'.[8] It had probably better be left out in translation. What Jesus wants to convey is that from now on any contact between him and his people will be of a different kind from what it was before.

The story in John 20: 19-23 is an appearance to the disciples. Here they do not receive the promise of the Spirit, as in Luke and Acts (Luke 24: 49; Acts 1: 8), but the Spirit is bestowed upon them there and then. To John the Spirit is the manner in which Christ is with his people after his resurrection (compare the discourses, John 13—16, especially 16: 12ff.). This is not an identity *tout court*, but does to some extent already point forward to the later Trinitarian dogma.[9]

At the same time they receive their apostolic commission. This entails the authority to forgive sins. The authority is a derived authority: they are to act in the name of Jesus, on his authority, by his command, on his behalf, but it is a real mandate. It is curious that verse 21 uses two different words for 'send', of which the first ('the Father has sent me') is connected with the word 'apostle', while the second ('I send you') is not, but this has probably no particular significance.

On that occasion Thomas was not present. He could not believe the story when he heard it. But eight days later the Lord showed himself again to the disciples, and Thomas got the opportunity to convince himself. We are not actually told that he touched the Lord, but we learn that he confessed him as 'my Lord and my God'. Three points should be noted. Thomas' confession is the result of his recognizing Jesus, not of any external proof (like touching him). He needed an answer, not to the question, *what* has appeared, but *who* has appeared. He asked for identification marks. Therefore it was enough for him to recognize the Lord.

Secondly, it is subtly indicated that Jesus was there even when the disciples did not see him: he had heard what Thomas had said.[10] And thirdly, Jesus' words to Thomas contain a certain criticism of the resurrection stories as such: the appearances should not have been necessary.[11]

6. THE APPEARANCE BY THE LAKESIDE

It is generally agreed that John 21 is an appendix to the Gospel. It is obvious that John 20: 30-31 was meant to be the end of the book. The questions arising from that are complicated by the fact that there is no difference in style between chapter 21 and the body of the Gospel, while the final paragraph (21: 24-25) distinguishes between the disciple, the witness who 'wrote the Gospel', and the 'we' who know that his testimony is reliable.

But whatever the answer to the question of authorship and the relation between John 1—20 and chapter 21, there is no doubt that the tradition embodied in this chapter is at variance with chapter 20. It has often been pointed out that the reference to the appearance by the lakeside as the third appearance is rather odd (21: 14). It is not true that chapter 20 already has three, because the appearance to Mary Magdalene was not one to the disciples. But the verse seems pointless unless there were some who did not regard this as the third appearance. The note of verse 14 is clearly meant to link this story, traditionally not regarded as the third appearance, to the two already described in chapter 20. But it seems highly unlikely that the tradition would count the Lord's appearances as no. 1, no. 2, no. 3, and so on. The only one that would be remembered with a figure attached would be the first. It is therefore not unreasonable to assume that the Evangelist received this story as the Lord's first appearance.

The contents of the story confirm that. If one reads John 21: 2-13 by itself there is nothing to suggest that Jesus was known to have been raised from the dead and had already appeared to his disciples. The situation is very much like that described in the Gospel according to Peter (Pseudo-Peter 58-60): 'When the last days of the feast of the Unleavened Loaves came, many left, returning to their homes, as the festival was over. But we, the twelve disciples of the Lord, wept and were full of sorrow. And everyone went to his home, grieved at what had happened. But I, Simon Peter, and Andrew, my brother, took our nets and went to the Lake; and with us was Levi, the son of Alphaeus, whom the Lord . . .' Here the fragment ends, but there can be little doubt that it leads up to some appearance of the Lord. We cannot know whether what followed resembled John 21, but the situation is very similar.

If this story, before it was added to the Fourth Gospel, circulated as an independent part of the tradition, and was told as a first appearance of the risen Lord, we have an answer to some awkward questions. The most obvious is, what were the disciples doing fishing in Galilee, if the Lord had already appeared to them in Jerusalem and sent them to proclaim the Gospel (John 20: 21-23)? The answer now becomes obvious: in the story as it was originally told they had not seen the risen Lord in Jerusalem.

The conversation between Jesus and Peter (21: 15-19) also is much easier to understand if we assume that the risen Lord had not appeared to Peter before.

The story of the miraculous draught of fishes occurs in Luke 5: 1-11 as well. A striking phrase in Luke's version is Peter's exclamation, 'Depart from me, for I am a sinful man, O Lord' (Luke 5: 8). Why this sudden confession? Is it because of Peter's awareness of something more than human?[1] Is it because repentance is called forth not by reproach but by God's goodness?[2] Or is it a reference to his denial? If the latter, then Luke's own version shows that he has it in the wrong context. It is a post-resurrection story (for Luke's reasons for putting it where he did, see page 22).

At the heart of the event is a meal of Jesus with his disciples. We are not actually told that he himself ate, only that he gave the bread and the fish to the disciples (verse 13). The early readers would be reminded of the Eucharist.

We are not told that Jesus gave the disciples any new information. The purpose of the appearance is a restoration of relationships. This comes about by a meal with all those present, and, in Peter's case, by dealing with some unfinished business between Peter and his Lord.

The restoration of the relationship between Christ and Peter entails his being reinstated in his apostolic office. Many interpreters seem to suspect some deep meaning in the variations used to describe this office: 'feed my lambs', 'tend my sheep', 'feed my sheep'. Others do the same in respect of the two words used for 'love'.[3] It is very doubtful whether the Evangelist had any such thing in mind. It simply belongs to the art of story-telling not to repeat the same phrase more than one can help. As to the Lord's intentions: he would not have used Greek at the time in any case.

The purpose of the addition of this chapter to the Gospel may have been partly to preserve a tradition which the final editor(s) thought worth preserving, partly to answer questions of the kind we find in verse 23.

7. PAUL TO THE CORINTHIANS

In 1 Corinthians 15: 3-8 the apostle Paul enumerates a number of the Lord's appearances after his resurrection. This, of course, is not a narrative of the resurrection but it does have some bearing on the matter in hand. Paul lists six appearances. This does not necessarily mean that he knew of no others, but it does seem likely that the enumeration of the first five was already traditional.

That the Lord first appeared to Peter is also mentioned in Luke 24: 34. As we saw (page 32) it is possible that the story in John 21 was originally told as a first appearance, and this could be called an appearance to Peter.

The Gospels contain several records of appearances to the Twelve.

The appearance to more than five hundred brethren cannot be identified with anything we find in the Gospels. It has been suggested that Paul may be referring to the events at Pentecost,[1] but our information is not sufficient for that kind of identification.

There is a reference to an appearance of the Lord to his brother James in the Gospel according to the Hebrews (recorded by Jerome, *De Viris Illustribus*, 2), but we do not know whether this is based on old tradition, nor indeed which James Paul had in mind (though the brother of Jesus was better known both to Paul and his readers).

The last appearance is one to Paul himself. He is referring to the appearance on the road to Damascus (Acts 9: 3-9; 22: 6-11; 26: 12-18; Galatians 1: 11-17), not to the one in the Temple (Acts 22: 17). Paul obviously regards the appearance on the road to Damascus as something entirely of the same kind as all the other appearances. Neither here nor in Galatians 1: 16 does Paul attempt to define the manner of the Lord's appearance. Luke varies his descriptions, but makes it clear every time that Paul's companions observed something but did not see the Lord.[2]

We should note that in this passage, which, of course, is much earlier than any of the Gospels, the belief in the resurrection of Christ is based solely on his appearances, not on the empty tomb. The latter is not even mentioned. It does not follow that Paul had not heard of it: one always has to be careful with the *argumentum e silentio*. And even if he knew no stories about the empty tomb he would still have taken it for granted that the grave was empty. But that makes the omission even more pointed. The empty tomb plays no part in Paul's Gospel because it is irrelevant to the belief in the risen Christ.

The construction of the passage bears that out. There are four finite verbs in two pairs, the first of each pair connected with the phrase 'in accordance with the scriptures', the second offering confirmation by the known facts. He 'died . . . in accordance with the scriptures', 'he was buried'; 'he was raised in accordance with the scriptures', 'he appeared'.[3] The faith in the risen Lord rests on his having appeared to his people.

Two more points ought to be noted. 'He was raised.' The resurrection of Christ is referred to in the passive voice. The resurrection of Christ is an act of God. Resurrection is not a continued activity of the human personality but God's new creation.

'And . . . he appeared.' The natural translation of the Greek is not, 'he was seen by . . .', but, 'he appeared to . . .' The emphasis is on the appearing, not on the seeing, not on what the disciples experienced but on what the Lord did to them.[4]

8. THE LONGER ENDING OF MARK

Two attempts have been made to give the Gospel according to Mark a more satisfactory ending. The shorter ending only rounds off the Gospel in a formal way and contains no information relevant to our subject.[1] The longer ending consists largely of what are apparently excerpts from the other Gospels.[2] But it is interesting to note that in 16: 14-18 it reports an appearance of the Lord while the Eleven sat at table, and that the Lord's words on this occasion are reminiscent of those in Matthew 28: 16-20. The date of the longer ending cannot be ascertained with any accuracy, but if the suggestion that it is ancient and may be as early as the beginning of the second century[3] is correct, it would not be impossible for it to contain independent tradition. It is just possible that verses 14-18 reflect a tradition in which the missionary command of Matthew 28: 16-20 was not connected with an appearance in Galilee.

9. SOME CONCLUSIONS

The narratives of the resurrection reflect various traditions, which fall into three groups. One is connected with the tomb, one with appearances in Jerusalem, and a third with appearances in Galilee.

The Epistles of Paul make no reference to the tomb tradition at all. In the earlier Gospels the story stands by itself. It is not connected with the appearances, and it does not lead to any belief in the resurrection.[1] John alone seems to connect the belief in the resurrection with the empty tomb, but even here we cannot be certain (see page 30).

The Galilean tradition does not appear in the sources until late. We have seen that the apparent reference to this tradition in Mark 16: 7 is doubtful (see page 19), and that we cannot be certain that Matthew 28: 16-20 is based on tradition (page 21). Only John 21 and Pseudo-Peter contain material that belongs undoubtedly to the Galilean tradition.

The growing together of those traditions has left us with an extremely complicated collection of stories. Several attempts have been made at unravelling the knots and arriving at an acceptable course of events. One can easily exaggerate the importance of such attempts. As oral tradition consists essentially of small units, it is rarely possible to force it into the framework of an historical scheme. On the other hand, whatever the nature of the appearances, the disciples must have been somewhere when the Lord appeared to them.

It has been suggested that the Galilean tradition is the product of pious fantasy.[2] F. C. Burkitt was an especially eloquent exponent of that view. His real point is that in order to accept the Galilean tradition we have to invent a return to Jerusalem. It is not a question of believing an old tradition but of inventing a new one, for the message to return to Jerusalem is not included in the tradition. The documents that tell us of appearances say nothing about returning to Jerusalem. Burkitt does not deny that the disciples, with Peter in the lead, left Jerusalem to go fishing. But he is convinced that they did not get very far. 'What if Peter saw the Lord on the way, before he had got far from the Holy City? Would it not make him retrace his steps?' He suggests that the *Quo vadis* legend contains an element of Jerusalem tradition.[3]

Had Galilee been the place of the Lord's appearances, would not Galilee have become the holy place of the Christians? But the Church at Jerusalem is a solid fact of history. This is the holy city of the Christian Church because it was here that they saw the risen Lord. The appearances in Galilee are postdated stories of earlier events.

But Burkitt's argument works both ways. That Jerusalem was the holy city of the Christians could also account for the arising of a Jerusalem tradition without any historical foundation. Moreover, there is evidence that Christianity was widespread in Galilee at an early date. That the New Testament does not contain any references to the origins of Galilean Christianity does not prove that there were no groups of Christians in Galilee as soon as the Church in Jerusalem came into being. The New Testament does not tell us anything about the origins of the Church in Rome either, and yet there can be no doubt that it must have started some time before Paul wrote his Epistle to the Romans.

It could be, and it has been, argued that the Galilean tradition is based on fact and the Jerusalem tradition on fiction.[4] Is it likely, if the followers of Jesus never left Jerusalem after the death of Jesus, that they would have invented a flight to Galilee?

But is it really necessary to choose? Is it not possible for both traditions to have a foundation in actual events?

We have to be clear on one point. The Gospels do not give us the kind of information that would make it possible to reconstruct the exact course of events with any certainty. That holds good of the resurrection stories even more than of

other parts of the Gospels.[5] Attempting any such reconstruction would imply a gross misjudgment both of the
character of oral tradition and of the strangeness of the
events.

Nevertheless it is not impossible to suggest, in very
general terms and without any attempt at precision, a course
of events which would account for the existence of both the
Galilean and the Jerusalem traditions. If the disciples stayed
at Jerusalem till the end of the festival, as suggested by
Pseudo-Peter 58-59, then it is not at all difficult to account
for both traditions, and for the tomb tradition as well.

And, of course, they had every reason to stay till the end
of the festival. No matter whether they were in a festive
mood, it would have been extremely imprudent to draw
attention to themselves by leaving the city while nobody else
did. There is no better hiding-place than a crowd.[6] While
they were there, the discovery of the empty tomb would
have been an insignificant incident, an unpleasant affair, a
riddle perhaps, but no more. Even Mary Magdalene's story
would not have seemed very significant to men who were
not distinguished by the high flight of their imagination.

There is no reason to assume that all the disciples left
Jerusalem at the end of the festival. Jesus had his followers
in Judea too, and there was no reason for them to join the
others, now that the whole affair was over and done with. It
would therefore have been possible and even likely for appearances to have taken place both in Galilee and in Jerusalem. Admittedly there is no tradition concerning the return
of the Galilean disciples to Jerusalem but that is scarcely
surprising considering both the fragmentary condition of the
tradition and its aim to be a witness to Christ, not a collection of anecdotes concerning the disciples.

Naturally, in time, knowing that the disciples had still
been in Jerusalem for some period immediately after the
death of Jesus, it would seem strange that the Lord had not
appeared to them before they fled. And, as there were
traditions concerning appearances in Jerusalem, it would

seem to stand to reason that they must have taken place soon after the crucifixion. They would first be placed before the disciples' flight to Galilee, then the flight would no longer be mentioned and eventually it would be entirely forgotten.[7]

We are not suggesting that that is how it must have happened or at any rate did happen. It is what may have happened. We have not the necessary evidence to reconstruct the order of events with any exactitude. There are probably several other possibilities. But so long as all the available evidence can be accounted for in some way or other it would be rash to discount any part of the evidence or reject it out of hand.

In considering questions of this kind one is always inclined to overlook that the links between the various parts of the tradition are a creation of the authors, and purely editorial. They are not arbitrary. And they are essential. Without them the author would not be able to write a book at all. As long as the tradition is handed down by word of mouth every unit can be told by itself. But as soon as one attempts to write a book one has to link the units in some way or other. It would be extremely silly to criticize the author for doing the one thing that enables him to turn the disjointed and unrelated parts of the tradition into a book. But the perspective dependent on those links varies with the authors and is different from that of a modern historian.

We must now have a look at the most controversial part of the evidence, the tomb tradition. Two reasons have been advanced why it must be late and unreliable. First of all that Paul does not refer to it. That does not necessarily mean that he did not know it. He may have known it and not regarded it as relevant. His not mentioning it proves neither one thing nor the other. Secondly, there are the words in the Gospel according to Mark, 'they said nothing to any one' (Mark 16: 8). They seem to indicate that there was a time when the story was not generally known, and to explain how that came about.[8] But there was an excellent reason why the story should not be broadcast while there was any danger

for the women concerned. The accusation that the grave
had been tampered with was levelled at the Christians at a
very early date. The admission that someone belonging to
the circle of the disciples had been at the grave early in the
morning could have given rise to the most unpleasant sus-
picions and might have been dangerous to those concerned.
Had the message of the empty tomb been in any way
essential to the belief in the resurrection, they would have
had no choice. But as that belief did not depend on an empty
tomb but on the living Lord having appeared to his disciples,
there was no reason to take unnecessary risks: the un-
avoidable risks were already serious enough without adding
to them.

Most people who object to the story, however, do so on
other than historical grounds. It is commonplace to say that
the story fits into an ancient view of the world but not into
ours. That is rather naïve. We have no monopoly of observ-
ing that people do not walk out of their graves. The ancient
world knew that as well as we do.

One may say that we do not need the empty tomb. It is
perfectly possible to believe in the resurrection of Christ and
yet be confident that his bones are still lying somewhere in
Israel.[9] Others are not so confident about that, but would
still maintain that Christ rose from the dead, no matter
what happened to the grave.[10] But then the Gospels already
knew that the empty tomb did not prove a thing. Both Paul
and the Evangelists knew that people believed, not because
something odd had happened about the Lord's grave but
because the risen Lord had appeared to his disciples.

Nevertheless it would be extremely difficult to object to
the grave story on purely historical grounds. Even if we
assume that it served the purpose of checking an incipient
grave cult,[11] that would not explain how the story arose in
the first place. Traditions may serve a particular purpose in
the community, but that does not necessarily mean that they
were invented for the purpose. Nevertheless, they can, and
often do, change with the needs of the communities they

serve. It should be noted that the Gospel according to Mark does not actually say that the grave was empty, only that it was open. It would be quite possible for the women to have had some experience when they approached the grave, a vision of an angel, perhaps even an appearance of the Lord himself (Matthew 28: 8-9); and afterwards, in view of the later experiences of the Christian community and the appearances of the risen Lord, the conclusion that the grave was empty must have seemed obvious. That, indeed, seems a very plausible and attractive suggestion, which would account for most of the available evidence.

However, in a world in which the Christian Church had many enemies, some of no mean intelligence, there is no evidence that anyone ever suggested that the body was still in the grave. It has been suggested that the early Church at Jerusalem did not preach the resurrection, so that the question did not arise. If that was so, it must have been a very closely guarded secret. We have no evidence that the Christian faith was ever preached without the resurrection. And what would have been easier for the authorities than to produce the body, had it been there? That would not have invalidated the message of the resurrection but it would have been extremely awkward. Instead great pains were taken to explain the empty tomb without the resurrection. That the tomb was empty does not at any time seem to have been a point of controversy. What Christians and their opponents disagreed about was how it came to be empty.[12]

Therefore the conclusion must stand that the story of the empty tomb cannot be easily dismissed. Yet it is only on the periphery of the message. The disciples believed in the risen Christ, not because they had seen an empty grave, but because he had met them.

We must finally mention the suggestion that the Easter stories only reflect an inner experience, especially at the Lord's Supper. That encounter with the Lord can be very real. When, for instance, Willem de Merode, in his poem '*Heilig Avondmaal*' ('The Lord's Supper'), writes,

> But their Lord, alive, stood in their midst,
> And their eyes, misted over with tears,
> Could not bear the splendour of his glory,[13]

he not merely reminds us of the biblical resurrection stories: had those words been written in the first century, they would no doubt have been regarded as referring to one of the Lord's appearances. But that, I submit, does not affect the reliability of the biblical accounts. It only underlines what the Church has always believed: that Jesus Christ is alive today as he was then. It does, however, remind us of the next inquiry we shall have to make, the inquiry into the nature of the event.

2

THE NATURE OF
THE EVENT

I. THE RESURRECTION OF CHRIST AND HISTORY

The conclusions of Chapter 1 lead naturally to the question of the historicity of the resurrection. We saw that the story of the empty tomb is presented in the Bible as an historical event. We cannot help feeling that the last word has not been said about that. But we also saw that the empty tomb is not regarded, except possibly in one case, as sufficient ground for the belief in the resurrection.

The appearances, on the other hand, can be safely regarded as historical events. This holds good, no matter how we interpret them. Spiritual experiences are as much part of history as physically observable events. Even if the 'seeing' of the disciples was purely imaginary, even if there never was a risen Lord, even if the experience of his appearances had no real object, the experience itself would still be an historical fact.

We must go one step further. That the appearances are an historical fact is still true, even if the events described in the Gospels are merely the reflection of the disciples' experience that their Lord was alive.

The question therefore is not whether the disciples' experiences were a fact of history but whether the resurrection of Christ itself was an event in history.

What actually do we mean when we call an event historical? The origin of the word 'history' cannot help us very much: it is derived from a verb meaning 'to find out'. We have not, in English, such convenient words as the German *Geschichte* and the Dutch *geschiedenis*, referring to 'that which happened'. History is in fact the study of past events, but with some qualification. It is usually confined to the study of past events among humans. At one time the use of the word was even further limited to such events as could be studied from written sources. But even if the word should be extended to cover as wide a field as possible, few would quarrel with the demand that it should be confined to such events as have taken place in space and time.[1] Not only our experience and all our experiments but indeed our very thinking is determined by the categories of space and time.[2] No 'history' can go further.

'History' is used both of the examination and study of past events, and of the events themselves. Properly speaking anything that cannot be approached by historical examination and study should not be classified as historical. That does not, of course, mean that events which cannot or have not yet been so approached are not historical, but it does exclude everything that cannot, on principle, be the subject of history as a discipline.

For centuries the fundamental attitude of the Western mind has been one of agnosticism: only that which can be known through experience and experiment can be relevant, because only that belongs to the world we know, the world we live in and are concerned with. It is only one step from there to the conclusion that only that which is so known is real: that reality is confined to the phenomenal world. That is not a necessary conclusion, it is not even a logical one, but it is one that is widely taken for granted. We are not suggesting that modern scholarship in general, and modern science in particular, is sold to this view. But it seems undeniable that the spiritual climate of our times is largely determined by it.

That means, for our subject, that only that which has happened in space and time, and which can, if not always in fact, at least on principle, be examined and verified by historical methods, in other words, that which is 'historical', can be true. Both traditional and liberal Christianity seem to have regarded that as axiomatic, and in this they only reflect the general mood of their time.

That is not affected by the fact that history differs from science not only in its subject but also in its aim and methods. Whereas science is concerned with that which by its nature is generally and universally valid and can be put to the test, history is concerned with what happened once and cannot be repeated under the same conditions. There is therefore a great difference between scientific and historical evidence. But both are concerned with the phenomenal world.

Traditional Christianity insists on the historicity of the resurrection: only if the resurrection of Christ was an event in history can there be any point in the gospel at all. That seems the most effective way of safeguarding the gospel message against a spiritualization which would eventually make it evaporate completely.

But the danger should be obvious. On the traditional assumption the resurrection of Christ is not only an historical event, but its historicity guarantees its 'truth'. The event is regarded as relevant because it is historical and therefore 'true'. That makes it possible to regard the Christian faith as no more than the belief that certain events have happened in history. It makes room for the misinterpretation of the Christian faith as the assertion of certain historical events.

The New Testament does not supply the material for the historical approach of the resurrection. It simply does not provide the evidence necessary to establish the resurrection of Christ as an historical event. And that is not just an incidental deficiency. The New Testament authors were witnesses to a living Christ who was a present reality. The risen Christ himself was the starting-point. His resurrection needed no proof any more than we expect a person whom we meet to prove to us that he was born.

Those who want evidence of an historical kind will be inclined to regard the Gospel tradition as deficient. That deficiency had been sensed at a very early date. Pseudo-Peter already attempts to supply the necessary. In paragraphs 35-44 we read how the soldiers guarding the tomb saw it all happen. That had two advantages. It established the resurrection as an observable event. And, as those soldiers were not themselves Christians and therefore not biased in favour of the resurrection, their testimony carried so much more weight.

The canonical Gospels contain nothing of the kind. The stories of the guard in Matthew and of the women at the tomb are the best the New Testament has to offer. But neither of them are much good as evidence of the resurrection. It is noteworthy that the guards in Matthew do not see the resurrection of Christ but only an angel, and it is inferred that they fled before they had even examined the grave. However, traditional Christianity has tried to make the best of a bad job by stressing the importance of the two stories to an extent entirely out of proportion with the very minor role they play in the New Testament.[3]

That does not mean that traditional Christianity regards the resurrection of Christ as a *proved* historical fact (whatever 'proved' may mean in this context). One may occasionally come across such daring and absurd statements as that the resurrection of Christ is the best accredited event in all history, but such assertions are rare. The usual position is far more careful but nevertheless insists on the historical reliability of the witnesses and the historical reality of the resurrection.

In that way the traditional writers wanted to guard the Christian faith against subjectivity and emotionalism. They wanted to give the Christian faith a solid foundation in the historical reality, the only reality we know.

The aim is laudable. The biblical message is emphatic that the resurrection of Christ is real beyond the experience of the believers. On the assumption that the historical reality is not only the only reality we know but that there is indeed no other, one must attempt to safeguard the reality of the resurrection, that is to say its historical reality.

To the biblical authors the question did not present itself in the same way. They had no definition of history, and thus they would not see the problem in this particular way. Pseudo-Peter shows that it was soon felt instinctively, and even the New Testament itself shows signs of that same instinct. But it could not be voiced deliberately and articulately. It is therefore useless to say that there is no evidence that the New Testament writers distinguished between the death of Jesus as an historical event and his resurrection as something that did not come within that category.[4] The biblical authors did not answer questions which neither they nor anybody else asked.

But that is not the last word on the biblical evidence. For there is one distinction they did make, one that is directly relevant to the matter in hand. They distinguished between the present age and the age to come. The age to come was God's time, which was to make an end of all human history. That does not mean that the age to come was regarded as 'eternal' in the sense of 'beyond time'. That would have been a philosophical distinction which would never have occurred to the biblical authors. The distinction was a practical one. The best way to distinguish between the two times is to speak of 'our time' and 'God's time'.[5] That distinction does not solve our problem. It merely pinpoints it. It can do no more than indicate the fundamental difficulty which one encounters if one wants to speak of the 'last things' at all. But in making this distinction one does at least say what the distinctive mark is of the age to come: it is that future that belongs to God.

Jewish eschatology and especially apocalyptics have attempted to give a description of events inaugurating the age to come, in terms of history. The result of such historicizing of the last things is that the coming of the age to come is mythologized. The New Testament is extremely sparing with that kind of thing. In spite of the eschatological colour of much in the New Testament it is generally extremely cautious in its descriptions. The great exception is the

Apocalypse of John, and even there we miss the point if we regard the book as a blueprint of events to come, a world history of the future. The thing that matters in New Testament eschatology is that God will not only reign[6] but will be seen to reign. The emphasis is clearly on what really is the essential and fundamental difference between the present age and the age to come.

There can be no doubt that Mark regarded the resurrection of Christ as an eschatological event: as something that belongs to the age to come. As we saw, that could be one good reason why he does not refer to the Lord's appearances. What could possibly follow after the end? He must have known of those appearances. And, of course, he knew that history had carried on after the resurrection of Christ, apparently very much as it had before. What problems, if any, that raised in his mind we shall never know, because he remains silent on the subject.

In pre-resurrection parts of the Gospel according to Mark there seems to be no clear dividing line between the Parousia and the resurrection. It is true that they are never mentioned together. But when either the Parousia or the resurrection of Christ is referred to, they have one thing in common. They are always the final event, the last thing, the *eschaton* in the full sense of the word. Thus we find that in the predictions of the passion and resurrection there is no mention of the Parousia. We need not now concern ourselves with the question whether Jesus did or did not predict his passion and resurrection. It does not seem at all unlikely that our Lord knew at a very early stage of his ministry what the outcome would be. And is it at all strange that he should have had the hope of the resurrection? At any rate, in the Gospel as it stands the predictions of his passion and resurrection play an important part. And in those predictions the Parousia is not mentioned: the resurrection of Christ itself is the last thing in the full sense, it is *the eschaton* (Mark 8: 31; 9: 31; 10:34). On the other hand passages referring to the Parousia (Mark 8: 38; 13: 26ff.; and we might add 9: 1; 14: 25) do not mention the resurrection. Mark 9: 1 has sometimes been interpreted as referring to the resurrection of Christ. This is certainly a misinterpretation, inspired, no doubt, by a desire to make all the Lord's words 'come true'. The words of Jesus in which he speaks of the Parousia and those in which he foretells his death and resurrection belong to two different contexts of association. But they are both referring to the *eschaton*.

The exception, a significant exception, is Mark 9: 9-10, the only place where something comes after the resurrection. Here the disciples are told to keep the story of the transfiguration to themselves until the Son of man should have risen from the dead. They wonder what the rising from the dead means. Surely the resurrection of the dead cannot have been an entirely unknown expression? But the resurrection of the dead is the *eschaton*, and what could be the point of telling the story *after the end of all history*?

The other Evangelists have tried to relate the resurrection of Christ more closely to history. Matthew does this by the story of the guard, though he refrains from actually describing the event of the resurrection. The angel does not open the tomb to let Jesus out but to let the women in. Moreover the Lord's final words (Matthew 28: 20) envisage a period of time 'to the close of the [present] age'.

Luke gives the appearances such substance that they assume the character almost of natural events. Maybe he wished to guard the message of the resurrection against over-spiritual interpretations. His insistence that Jesus was not a 'ghost' (Luke 24: 36-43) seems to suggest this, even though the emphasis is on the identity of the Lord rather than on the nature of the appearance.

In the ascension story (Acts 1: 6-11) the Parousia very definitely becomes a second event, separated in time from the resurrection. The story suggests, though it does not actually relate, the ending of a myth of the divine son of God having come to earth and having lived and died and risen, all in history, finally leaving for 'heaven'. The ascension is not actually described as an upward journey (see page 27) but the suggestion is there.

But the story of the men on the road to Emmaus presents an entirely different picture. Here the resurrection of Christ is referred to as Jesus entering into his glory (Luke 24: 26). Not only is the resurrection here equated with the ascension but surely the 'glory' can scarcely be regarded as a proper object of historical inquiry. Should we, regardless of this, look at the story from the 'historical' point of view suggested by the Acts, then the whole story becomes extremely awkward. The walk of Jesus together with the men, their conversation, the invitation to stay, the beginning of the meal, all that could fit in quite nicely with an historical understanding of the resurrection. But where did Jesus come from? Where did he go when they saw him no longer? 'Historically' speaking the answer would be, nowhere. The proper answer, of course, is into 'the glory'. But this can scarcely be considered a place in the ordinary accepted sense of the word. In the Gospel the question is not asked and therefore not answered. For the important question is, who is he? But we have asked the question, and the only possible answer is non-historical.

The Gospel according to John presents its own peculiar difficulties. The Evangelist does not merely relate stories about Jesus and record some of the words he spoke while in the flesh, but interprets them, as we would say, in the light of many years of Christian experience. We should hasten to add that the Evangelist would have regarded this as a gross misinterpretation of his intentions. He interpreted the words and actions of the Lord while he was on earth in the light of the words of the risen Christ, conveyed through the Spirit (compare John 16: 7-15, and especially 14: 22-26). That should make us careful when we read that the Beloved Disciple believed when he looked into the grave (see page 30 on this passage). In the Gospel according to John 'to be-lieve' without any mention of the object usually refers to faith in the full sense of the word.[7] That makes it unlikely that the verse should mean, 'he believed that the body was gone'. Neither does it mean, 'he believed that Jesus had risen': it means more than that but includes it. There can be no doubt that to the Evangelist, faith in the full sense of the word includes the belief in the resurrection of Christ.[8] But how much of John 20: 8 is actual reminiscence, and how much is due to reading later experience back into the story?[9] Or, in other words, how much is report, and how much is, in the Evangelist's understanding, the Lord's interpretation?

In the stories of the appearances, John, like Luke, gives the events considerable substance. Mary Magdalene is told not to hold the Lord (John 20: 17), which infers that she was holding him. The Lord shows the disciples his wounds (20: 20). Thomas is invited to touch him, though we are not actually told that he did (20: 27-28). Yet there is a hint that the appearances should not have been necessary, that the risen Lord should be believed without being seen (20: 29; see also page 32).[10]

In the appendix the Parousia is referred to as a separate event (John 21: 22).

Paul too, in 1 Corinthians 15, refers to the resurrection of Christ and the Parousia as two distinct events.

Paul, in this account of the resurrection, does not use the argument of the empty tomb. We cannot tell whether or not he knew the story but it obviously played no part in his belief in the resurrection. That belief has two roots. First of all there are the Scriptures. Actually nothing of the kind is foretold in the Old Testament, though some passages (Psalm 49: 15; 73: 26; Isaiah 53: 10-12, and others) may have been interpreted as relating either to the resurrection of the dead in general or to the resurrection of the Suffering Servant. But there is a pattern in God's ways in the Old Testament that leads straight to the passion and resurrection of Christ (cf. page 25 on Luke 24).[11] Paul's second, and main, argument is that Jesus appeared. But not only is no attempt made to define the manner of the appearances, let alone the manner of seeing, but Paul actually equates some appearances which, according to Luke at least, belong to entirely different categories. There is no doubt that Luke regarded the appearances before the ascension as having had some kind of physical substance, whereas the appearance to Paul was a vision (Acts 26: 19). Had Luke's vocabulary stretched to it he might have called it an 'objective vision'. He stresses its objective character, once by saying that the men travelling with Paul heard the voice but saw no one (Acts 9: 7), once by telling us that they saw the light but did not hear the voice (22: 9). In both cases, though by different means, Luke wants to convey the same thing: that the appearance was a vision but that it did not originate in Paul's own imagination, it was a real objective event.[12] Even so he regarded it as different in kind from the appearances before the ascension. Paul, on the other hand, does not inquire into the kind, and makes no distinctions. His question is not, how, or what, but who. This, of course, was also Luke's main question. But it was Paul's only question. This seems rather a cavalier treatment of what would be essential, if the resurrection is to be regarded as an historical event. It is true that our particular line of inquiry would not have occurred to Paul but that is itself significant. He disregards precisely the point that is essential as historical evidence for a resurrection in history.

The point of Paul's argument in this chapter is not that he wants to prove that Jesus Christ was raised from the dead. The chapter deals with the general resurrection, and his point is that the resurrection of Christ presupposes the general resurrection. His readers needed no convincing that Jesus Christ was raised from the dead. What they doubted was the general resurrection: it was the end, the *eschaton*, that was in question. Paul argues that if there is no such *eschaton*, if there is no resurrection of the dead, then Christ was not raised (1 Corinthians 15: 13). The real meaning of 1 Corinthians 15 is not that the Lord's appearances are evidence of his resurrection (though this is implied) but that the resurrection of Christ is evidence of the general resurrection and therefore of the *eschaton*, the end, the limit of history. The appearances mean that this limit has been seen.[13] Inquiring into how this has been seen is absurd, just as absurd as asking how the dead rise (1 Corinthians 15: 35-36).[14]

Paul's approach differs from Mark's but is nevertheless very close to it. These two earliest witnesses wrote before the need of historical evidence arose. Resurrection to them is the *eschaton*, the end. The conclusion we must draw, even if they did not, is that the resurrection cannot be an event *in history*. Had it been in history it would have been its final event. The resurrection is obviously not the end of history in an 'historical' sense. It is the *eschaton* in another, far more radical, sense.

Throughout the history of the Church, Luke has had more disciples than Mark and Paul, and many attempts have been made to fit the resurrection and the Parousia of Christ into a neat historical scheme. Among recent attempts we mention the brilliantly devised schemes of F. W. A. Korff[15] and Oscar Cullmann.[16]

The most obvious difficulty for such schemes is that we have not the kind of historical evidence needed to establish the resurrection of Christ as an event in history. The same holds good even more, naturally, of the Parousia; but that has its compensations: no one can check us if we want to write a world history of the future. But, apart from the dim view the whole of the Bible takes of prying into the future, is that really what the hope of the Parousia is about?

All that touches only the surface. Much more serious is that by classifying the resurrection of Christ as an historical event we do not do justice to its true nature. The resurrection of the dead is the end of history, the *eschaton* in the full sense of the word. The resurrection of Christ is his entering into the glory (compare Luke 24: 26; Acts 1: 9; Philippians 2: 9-11). The glory is the manner in which God exists. It cannot be equated with the manner in which the world and we ourselves exist. Nor should the glory of God be regarded as an extension of the universe. It is not only of another quality and altogether different in kind but its very existence cannot be paralleled, let alone equated with our own existence. It is real, he is real, in a totally different sense from ourselves.

Theology has long been plagued by the implications of the *analogia entis*: God and the world have this in common, that they both exist. The concept has more to do with Hellenic, especially Aristotelian, thought[17] than with the Bible. If we must use such words about God as that he is, or exists, or that he is real, then we should remember that we use words connected with our ordinary experience only for lack of better. When speaking about God we should mean rather more than we could possibly say.

Therefore, if we consider it undesirable to regard the resurrection of Christ as an historical event, we do not deny that it is a real event, a real act of God. But its reality is different in kind from the ordinary historical reality, different in kind from any reality in the phenomenal world. The resurrection of Christ has obvious connexions with history. But the vessel of history is incapable of containing it.

One more point. It is widely thought that positive historical evidence of the resurrection would make faith unnecessary. It would actually make faith impossible. For faith is not the belief that certain things happened to Jesus. Such a belief is indeed connected with the Christian faith. But it is not identical with it. The Christian faith is a relationship with Jesus Christ. Even the Gospel according to Luke, which goes furthest in trying to historicize the resurrection of Christ, makes it clear that the decisive point is that the disciples recognized the Lord. This recognition implies the resurrection, and Luke and John especially have spoken of the resurrection as concretely, one might almost say as massively, as they could. But the all-important thing remains, not that the disciples came to believe certain things about Jesus, but that they recognized their risen Lord. In the final resort Christians believe in the risen Lord, and only

by implication in the resurrection. The crucial question remains, not, what do we believe about him, but in whom do
we believe?

2. RESURRECTION AND ESCHATOLOGY

We have so far referred to the resurrection of Christ as an
eschatological event. We shall now have to see if this is
adequate.

The man who has probably done more than anyone else
to show the eschatological character of the New Testament is
Albert Schweitzer, on whose work all who came after him
are dependent. He emphasizes that in the New Testament
the resurrection of Christ is an eschatological event. 'Resurrection of those who had died was only to take place when
the supernatural age had dawned. If Jesus has risen, that
means, for those who dare to think consistently, that it is
now already the supernatural age. And this is Paul's point of
view. . . .'[1] Through the resurrection of Jesus it had become
manifest that resurrection powers, that is to say, powers of
the supernatural world, were already at work within the
created world. . . . Behind the apparently immobile outward
show of the natural world, its transformation into the supernatural was in progress, as the transformation of a stage goes
on behind the curtain.'[2]

This view, which one can read in many variations, has the
great disadvantage that it makes the resurrection of Christ
part of a great cosmic drama, in which admittedly he plays
the title role but in which he has to abide by the script. It is
significant that the Gospels refrain from putting the resurrection of Christ in a wider eschatological framework.
Wherever such an eschatological context is found, reference
may be made to his Parousia, not to his resurrection. On the
other hand, where the resurrection is referred to, it
is always *the eschaton*, not part of a larger eschatological
drama.

This has been attributed to an error on the part of Jesus

or his hearers. They did not realize that the Parousia would
not coincide with his resurrection.[3] But this does not explain
why the two contexts of association are always kept apart.
If the resurrection and the Parousia had been consciously
and deliberately, though mistakenly, identified, one would
expect that sometimes at least the resurrection of Christ
would appear in a larger eschatological context, instead of
the Parousia. But that is not the case, precisely because they
belong to two different contexts of association. The Parousia,
which, incidentally, is a coming, an epiphany, an advent,
not a 'coming again', belongs to an inherited eschatological
framework. The resurrection of Christ as presented in the
gospel does not fit into such a framework. It is a new message.[4] For the eschatological drama is thought of as somehow a continuation of history, whereas the resurrection of
Christ is the *eschaton* in a far more fundamental sense. In the
sense of a final act of a cosmic drama the eschatological expectation has not been fulfilled and never will be fulfilled.[5]
But Jesus Christ was raised from the dead.

One of the characteristics of the New Testament message
is that the coming of God did *not* take place in the form of a
cosmic drama but in the human life of Jesus Christ, and that
God is with us in him, the risen Lord. Any references in the
New Testament to the future must be read against the background of that fundamental truth. The misinterpretations to
which especially the Revelation of John has often been ex-
posed come largely from reading the New Testament without
that insight.

In this context it is surely relevant that Jesus never referred
to himself as the Messiah. 'The kingdom of God' does not
necessarily refer to the messianic Kingdom, either as an
event in history or as a cosmic catastrophe. That God is
King, now, is surely one of the basic assertions of the Old
Testament. The succession stories in I Samuel evolve round
the question, who is the right *nagid*, governor, not, who is the
right *melekh*, king, of Israel?[6] The question can only be
answered in the light of the knowledge that Israel can have

no *melekh*, no king like the other nations (1 Samuel 8: 5) because YHVH is the King of Israel. The whole of the Old Testament is full of this fundamental insight.

It is therefore no radical reinterpretation when Jesus asserts that the Kingdom, the kingly rule of God is right here ('in the midst of you', Luke 17: 21). What is new is the implication that God's royal government is exercised through Jesus Christ, and that he is not merely a messenger but in some way identified with God's kingdom, that he is the *autobasileia*.

But the real difference between the New Testament and eschatology past and present is that eschatology is interested in *what* is coming, whereas the New Testament is interested in *who* has come. Surely the Christian faith is not that certain events have taken place in the past, nor the Christian hope that certain events will take place at some undetermined time in the future, but that Jesus Christ has come and that, whatever may happen, and wherever the road may lead, he will be there.

3. RESURRECTION AND MYTH

The rejection of history and eschatology as proper terms for the resurrection of Christ, the inadequacy of these as vehicles for the message of the resurrection, makes it tempting to regard it as a myth. The notion of myth has been very much in the forefront of theological thinking ever since Bultmann raised the problem of the need to demythologize the New Testament. The discussion has unfortunately often lost its way in cosmological questions. The emphasis is on the 'mythological understanding of the world', the 'mythological world-view', the 'mythological cosmogony', of the New Testament authors. It is obvious that these are no longer acceptable to modern man. It should be equally obvious that they belong to the language in which the New Testament authors had to express themselves, the only language they knew (see page 64).

However, that is not what makes a myth. It is not easy to define what actually does make a myth. Definitions vary greatly, and it is not surprising that the word has been used by such very different theologians as Reitzenstein,[1] Bousset,[2] Barth,[3] Brunner,[4] Bultmann,[5] and Tillich.

Myth distinguishes itself both from that which is merely historical and from mere speculation.[6] It attempts to reach beyond the historical reality, to get to the ground and fountainhead of history and indeed of all existence. But its manner is plastic, not speculative. It would be a mistake to think that myth has no reality for its object. Indeed, one might say that 'reality' is precisely what distinguishes myth from fiction.[7] But it has its eye fixed on a reality which is more than immanent and which, from the point of view of history, has an irrational character.[8] 'Myth is seen as a symbol, built up from elements of reality, for the Absolute, the being beyond beings, which is the object of the religious act',[9] a form of presentation which, reaching beyond the means of philosophical analysis and synthesis, attempts to express in a plastic figure that which cannot be said.[10] All those definitions make important points, but the main characteristic of a myth is that it presents an actual and present truth in the form of a story from the past.

Telling the myth is not mere reflection but an actual event. When the myth is told, the past is not merely remembered nor is the present truth merely contemplated: a truth is actualized and becomes a reality in the word.[11]

The story of a myth need not be 'mythical': it can also be an actual historical event. Few people would doubt that the Last Supper of our Lord with his disciples was such an actual historical event. One may wonder what its precise character was, one may question details of the biblical accounts, one may wonder if the words recorded in the Gospels were actually spoken on that occasion. But few would doubt that the Supper itself was an event in history.

But the repetition of the words of the institution at the Eucharist is not just the reading of a story from the past. Its

function in the liturgy is that it calls the Lord to be present
at this celebration. Whatever views one may hold of the
Lord's presence, there is no Church that teaches his real
absence.[12] In the liturgy therefore the words of the institution function as a myth.

In this sense the message of the resurrection of Christ also
functions as a myth. The resurrection of the Lord is not told
merely as a story from the past. It is an attempt to present
the risen Lord. What is important is not that people should
learn what happened to Jesus at some time in the past but
that they should be confronted with the living Lord.

Sometimes the presentation of the living Lord not only
functions as a myth but actually takes the form of a myth.
Though his resurrection is not mentioned in so many words,
the hymn quoted Philippians 2: 6-11 means to present the
risen Lord. Its form is mythological and related to the myth
of the god-man. It can easily be demonstrated that not only
here, but in other presentations of the risen Lord too, some
elements can be traced back to Jewish apocalyptic or
Hellenistic mythology.[13]

This, more than the difficulties presented by ancient cosmology, gives particular urgency to the problem of demythologizing the New Testament. If we should find that
the message of the resurrection not only functions as a myth
and is sometimes presented in the form of a myth, but is
actually borrowed lock, stock and barrel from contemporary
mythology, then we shall have to review our entire understanding of the Christian message radically. It would also
mean that there is a complete break between the faith of
Israel as presented in the Old Testament and the Christian
Church.

The myths which concern us here are either the resurrection myths of the Mystery religions or the Gnostic myth or
myths of redemption.

The first belong entirely to the sphere of the natural
world. The absolute and transcendent of which Tillich and
Gressmann speak is no more than the real nature of the

phenomenal world. It remains the natural world, but interpreted as divine. This is precisely what the Mystery myths
celebrate, the divine, eternal life of nature. In the Mystery
religions the resurrection belongs to the divine-natural
order of things: it is something that follows naturally.
Admittedly nature was more mysterious to the ancient mind
than it is to ours, but this does not affect the fundamental
point. Even when the Mystery religions promise 'eternal
life', this eternal life is the fruit of being initiated into the
eternal life of nature.

This whole religious complex is nothing to be sneered at.
But it is foreign to the faith of Israel. The identification of
God and nature is foreign to the relationship between
YHVH and his people as expressed in the Bible.

The same holds good of Gnosticism both in its monistic
and its dualistic forms. In its doctrine of man the human
spirit is always in some way or other an extension of the
Pleroma, the divine fullness, the divine essence. Eternal life
is already man's: he only has to realize it. The spirit of man
is *naturally* divine. Gnosticism knows nothing of the biblical
message that God is God and man is man.

The attempt to mythologize the resurrection of Christ has
probably been carried furthest by P.-L. Couchoud. In his
view it would be naïve to think that myths are necessarily
attached to any real fact. In that case Euhemerism would
explain all the gods. Osiris must have been an ancient
pharaoh, Attis some shepherd from Phrygia, Adonis a
Canaanite page-boy, Demeter an Aegean peasant woman.
That would be doubting unjustifiably the supremely creative
genius of religion, if one were to believe that man could not
have imagined a god Jesus if a man called Jesus had not
existed first.[14] Only the risen Jesus is historical.[15] He is not
the founder of a religion but a new god.[16]

It is awkward for this kind of interpretation that the
sources know nothing of a risen Christ other than the one
who was crucified recently 'under Pontius Pilate'. The
Gospel according to Mark in particular, when writing about

'Jesus Christ, the Son of God', gives us the picture of a thoroughly human life that can be regarded as other than merely human only by implication. Not only Mark but the whole of the New Testament insists on the identity of the glorified Son of God with the historical Jesus, with the *man* Jesus.

This identity has always been the crux of all Christology. This holds good not only of the later Christological dogma but also of the New Testament itself. But in the New Testament it is never put in question. And it is this identity which makes the use of the word 'myth' highly unsatisfactory.

Myth describes that which always is or always happens (though even that which 'always happens' leaves things as they were before). A myth is a particular way of speaking of the eternal life of nature or the eternal life of the soul (which is also nature of a kind) or just of eternal truths. The story of the resurrection speaks of something *einmalig*, that happened once and for all. Some who have recognized that still like to use the term 'myth' but with a particular slant. Helmut Thielicke insists that there is a genuine historical basis under the mythological phenomenon. Therefore the myth is not the objective exteriorization of a purely subjective inner experience: it is the subjective realization of a saving event which is itself objective.[17]

Emil Brunner speaks of the Christian myth but adds that it is unique in being an historical myth. The reality of which the Christian myth speaks, that is the person of Jesus Christ, is an historical reality.[18] But why does he use the word 'myth' for what he obviously regards as an historical event?

In this connexion we should also mention Rudolf Bultmann. His position, however, is fundamentally different from that of the mythological interpreters of the New Testament. For Bultmann the Christian message concerns a decisive saving act of God. He certainly does not regard that act of God as a myth. The whole point of demythologizing the New Testament is precisely to recognize the message in the mythological garb in which it is presented and free it from its mythological presentation.

According to Bultmann the Christian kerygma is presented in the New Testament in mythological form. One can disagree as to the extent to which that is the case but there is no doubt that it is frequently presented in the form of the myth of the god-man: 'was man, became god, suffered pains, gained heaven'.[19] Not only is it presented with certain motifs borrowed from mythology. If that were the case we could easily segregate the true gospel from its mythological accretions (as a previous generation thought). But the message itself often, though not always, comes in the form of a myth and frequently functions as one. The task of demythologizing is not one of sifting but of translation. The problem of demythologizing is one of hermeneutics.

In some form or other this problem arises whenever one translates a work from one language into another. It is simply not true that 'the French have a word for it'. They often do not. And this does not only apply to single words which sometimes have to be circumscribed: it holds good even more of patterns of thought. This explains why precisely the most exciting books are often untranslatable, or at least become very dull in translation, and also why sometimes an argument that is perfectly coherent in one language may become entirely unconvincing in another.

But this becomes even more serious when a message has to be translated from one world of experience and thought into another. This kind of translation may well reduce the message to an abstraction. And it cannot be denied that this danger has become acute in some demythologizers.

Yet Bultmann is right that the gospel sets forth that which is not of this world in terms of this world. But it is the contention of the gospel that this is not a bright idea of the New Testament authors but an act of God. The doctrine of the incarnation may at times be expressed in mythological form, but it stresses, rightly, that when in Jesus Christ we are confronted with God this is not merely a subjective experience

of the believers but an act of God. In Jesus Christ God's
revelation takes place, that is to say, God sets forth himself
in terms of this world.

4. RESURRECTION AND COSMOLOGY

The relation between the gospel and ancient cosmology has
already been referred to in passing (page 58). We shall now
have a closer look at it.

The problems connected with this relation have drawn a
good deal of attention recently through the work of Rudolf
Bultmann and his school. But the problems themselves are
not new. Nineteenth-century theology in particular was
constantly engaged precisely with those problems.

It goes without saying that the Christians of the first
century shared the views of their contemporaries as regards
the structure of the cosmos. This was the language of their
time, in which they had to think and to express themselves if
they wanted to speak and think at all. Neither they nor anybody else knew any other. Even if it had pleased God to
reveal to the biblical authors some cosmological information
unknown to their contemporaries they would still not have
been able to understand this information, let alone communicate it to others, for neither they nor their readers knew
a language in which such information could be expressed.
However, there is no evidence that God did anything so
absurd.

A point that seems to have fired the imagination particularly is that the biblical authors take the three-tier
universe for granted. The earth is flat, under the earth is the
underworld, and over the earth is the vault of heaven, with
God somewhere 'up there'. This view has been antiquated
for centuries, and to most people the God 'up there' has
become, first a God 'out there', and eventually a God
'beyond'.[1]

Some have taken that very literally. Thus Lavater wrote
(in 1769), 'A cannon ball would have more than a trillion

years ... to hurry away to the nearest fixed star ... One can imagine with what speed Jesus ascended to heaven'.[2] But that is not the attitude of mainstream theology, nor indeed of the New Testament. The New Testament authors accept the current view of the world but do not emphasize it; they use it very much in the same way in which we say that the sun rises. Of course, we are perfectly aware that it is the earth that moves, and not the sun—which they were not— but neither they nor we are talking in terms of cosmology at all. The ascension of Jesus is not told to communicate some cosmological information, and the fact that Luke thought of heaven as a place 'up there' is of no consequence. How unimportant it was, even to Luke himself, is shown by the fact that the cloud is not regarded as a vehicle to take Jesus up but as a symbol of God's glory. Naturally, when artists started to depict the scene visually, that changed. After all, there is only one way to present the scene pictorially. Space (the flat space of a wall or canvas—even perspective does not alter this fundamentally) is the language of pictorial art, and the language demands certain conventions. It is only the fact that we are too used to this type of presentation which makes us forget that the conventions of the art are part of its language, and that the medium determines the presentation. However, one can scarcely regard the conventions of visual art as adequate theological pronouncements. Artists do sometimes manage to convey the message of the gospel better than theologians. But it is unwise to disregard the fundamental difference between the media employed.

It is therefore not surprising that this particular point has never been a great obstacle to the Christian faith. It has been a useful topic for argument, but that is a different matter altogether. The transition from a God 'up there' to a God 'out there' to a God 'beyond', a God in something 'comparable to another dimension',[3] was made painlessly because it did not affect anything intrinsic to the Christian faith. Not all would have gone so far as Luther, who insisted that heaven is not a place,[4] but few would have quarrelled with the insight that what is important about heaven is not whether or not it is a place but that it is the manner in which Christ now exists.

If God suffers from any housing shortage, it is one of a different kind. It is not that we cannot find a place for him in the physical universe (we know that he needs no such place) but that we cannot fit him in in a far more fundamental sense. In traditional Christian thinking God is regarded as the prime mover of the universe. It has even been suggested that, as the universe demands such a prime mover, the universe itself was evidence of the 'existence' of God. Today we no longer need such a prime mover. We no longer need God as an hypothesis to explain the universe.[5] And we have no real evidence, evidence of the kind the scientist demands, that God is working in the universe.

We have to be quite clear what this means. It means, in fact, exactly what it says. We have no need of God as an hypothesis to explain the universe. We have no evidence of his working in the universe. And consequently he is not accessible to the methods of modern science. But the popular view of the world maintains something entirely different. Popular cosmology operates with 'laws of nature' which are not, as in science, working hypotheses. They are regarded as normative: not as describing what is, but as prescribing what must be. The nineteenth century, generally speaking, thought, quite sincerely, that this followed from the observation of natural phenomena. The student of philosophy will not find it difficult to detect the influence both of earlier Western philosophy (Descartes and Spinoza) and of Taoism.

This view of the world is as mythical as that of the biblical authors. And it was already outdated before it became popular. It had already been exploded by the critical philosophy of Kant. This did not prevent it from acquiring a tremendous following which as yet shows no sign of diminishing. But the belief in this nature pantheism is not based on scientific evidence but on a decision on another level, a religious decision. Neither theology nor science can benefit from the introduction of pantheistic mythology into the work of either.

This does not detract from the fact that in the phenomenal world no experiment has ever so much as hinted at the reality of God or at the resurrection of Christ. This holds good of psychical research as much as any other branch of knowledge. And this, of course, is precisely what one might expect if God is, indeed God. If God is God then he cannot be the object of scientific any more than historical investigation. If Jesus Christ is indeed, not a corpse that walked out of his grave, but the living Lord, we cannot expect to find him along the lines on which we examine the phenomenal world. It would be absurd to seek the living among the dead: as absurd as trying to prove 'that God exists'.

5. RESURRECTION AND IMMORTALITY

The negative results we have so far arrived at seem to make it necessary to find the answer in another direction. Traditionally this has been sought in the belief in the reality, pre-eminence and immortality of the spiritual, or at least the non-material. In the Christian Church this has found expression in the belief in the immortality of the soul.

The immortal soul has been part of Christian belief almost, though not quite, from the beginning. The non-material and independent nature and existence of the soul implies its immortality. The soul only uses the body as an instrument. The destruction of the instrument does not necessarily entail the destruction of the user. Moreover, the soul, being non-material, is indivisible and can therefore not be dissolved into its component parts. It must therefore be indestructible. The Fifth Lateran Council declared the doctrine of the immortality of the soul a dogma of the Church.[1]

Roman Catholic theology has consistently maintained this, and not until recently was the question asked whether immortality is really the best way to express the Christian hope.[2]

Protestant theology does not present quite the same picture. Luther founded his hope on other grounds and did not think much of the doctrine.[3] Calvin accepted it[4] but some of his followers attempted to guard it against misunderstanding. 'The human soul is immortal, not unqualified, as if God could not reduce it to nothing, but by God's will, and because nothing other than God can destroy it.'[5] Nevertheless, though the soul is immortal only by God's will, this immortality is part of man's natural make-up, the soul is immortal *per naturam*.[6] The Scripture, it is maintained, teaches clearly and indisputably man's immortality.[7] However, protests have not been lacking. We mention such names as J. H. Gunning, G. van der Leeuw,[8] Walter Künneth,[9] and especially Karl Barth.[10]

In spite of Bavinck's assertion that the Scripture teaches clearly and indisputably man's immortality, it is scarcely necessary to demonstrate that no part of the Old or the New Testaments teaches anything of the kind. The word 'immortal' is not found in the Bible, the noun 'immortality' only three times, in 1 Corinthians 15:53-54 and 1 Timothy 6:16. In 1 Timothy 6 immortality is something that God alone has, in 1 Corinthians 15 it is something that man does not have but may be given.

That is in accordance with ancient Semitic tradition. 'You will never find the life for which you are looking. When the gods created man they allotted to him death; life they kept to themselves.'[11] Death is the end, even though it is not regarded as mere nothingness.[12]

In the Old Testament the realization that death is death and dead is dead is coloured by the knowledge that the living God, the God of Israel, has life and death in his hands. God reveals himself to Israel as the Free One, and no one would dream of snatching the secret of life from him.[13] But he is also the One who loves his people. Life is a free gift of God's love, and in his own good time he takes it back. Both life and its appointed end are meaningful. When life has come to full fruition, man dies, in good old age (Genesis 15: 15), old and satisfied with years (Genesis 25: 8). There is nothing tragic about that. Man has played his part in God's plan, he has enjoyed all that God gave him to enjoy, and all is well. Only when people die 'before their time', when they are not of ripe old age and satisfied with years does the believer sense something of the tragedy of death. This explains the many prayers for deliverance from death, especially in the Psalms (for example Psalm 6: 5; 88: 10-11; but also Isaiah 38: 18).

Occasionally we find some surprise that the relationship of love and faith between God and the faithful does not last for ever: 'Turn, O Lord, save my life; deliver me for the sake of thy steadfast love. For in death there is no remembrance of thee; in Sheol who can give thee praise?' (Psalm 6: 4-5). The Israelite knows that the Lord is more powerful than death. Wherefore then does he allow man to be swallowed up by Sheol?

Sheol, the realm of the dead (Hades in the New Testament) is not what we call 'hell', and even less what we call 'heaven'. In Sheol one does not live, let alone have eternal life. In Sheol one is dead. What that means no one knows but it is certainly nothing like being alive.

The idea of a natural immortality is not found in the Old Testament.[14] What could be immortal? Everybody knows that the body perishes. And what about the soul? But the Old Testament does not know such a thing as a separate soul. However we like to translate *nefesh*, 'life', or 'living being', or even 'soul', it is never regarded as something apart from the body. It is not something in man but it is that which defines him as a living creature. Therefore it is not unusual to read that the *nefesh* dies. It simply means that this particular living being dies. The Old Testament writers would have regarded the idea that the body dies and the soul lives on as quite absurd. Death strikes man in his entirety.

Only on two occasions is it said expressly in the Old

Testament that someone did live on: it is said of Enoch (Genesis 5: 24) and of Elijah. Outside the Old Testament a similar belief arose about Moses. Therefore anyone returning to this earth must be one of those three (compare John 1: 25; Mark 9: 1-8). The belief itself need not concern us. But it is relevant to the subject in hand that in all three cases the legend took the form that the body could not be found.

The same holds good of the New Testament. To be sure, the New Testament was written in a language in which *psyche*, 'soul', was normally used in the sense of something *in* man, something distinct from the body. It is therefore inevitable that the authors sometimes lay themselves open to misunderstanding. Yet it is really amazing how rarely that happens, especially in the Gospels [15] and in Paul's letters.[16] There is little doubt that passages like 1 Thessalonians 5: 23 and Revelation 6: 9, if pressed,[17] could be interpreted as referring to the soul as something distinct from the body. It is, however, doubtful if they should be so interpreted, and, generally speaking, the New Testament uses the word *psyche* in exactly the same sense as the Old Testament uses *nefesh*, to define man as a living being.

It is therefore not surprising that the resurrection of Christ found the disciples totally unprepared. Where there is a belief in a natural immortality, an immortality of the soul, a survival of the personality, it is not difficult to believe that the surviving personality may manifest itself somehow or other. But to the disciples Jesus was dead and gone. As far as they were concerned that was the end of the road; they knew of no road beyond death.

Admittedly by that time a belief in the resurrection of the dead had become fairly widespread in Israel. But that was precisely not a belief in the continued existence of the soul. Resurrection of the dead meant a new creation of the whole man. And it was an eschatological notion. It was expected as an act of God in the age to come, not now. Immortality or survival would be part of a doctrine of man which the Bible rejects: resurrection belongs to the doctrine of God.

That the resurrection of Christ was regarded as an act of God and not as the continuation of his former existence is borne out by the vocabulary of the New Testament. The Greek for 'rise' is used ten times of the resurrection of Christ, whereas the words for 'raise' or 'being raised' occur fifty-eight times in that connexion.[18] We are not suggesting that that was deliberate. But an unconscious preference is even more significant than a deliberate choice. The standing word for the resurrection, it is true, is a noun derived from 'rise' (one derived from 'raise' is found only in Matthew 27: 53), but not only was the word already in common usage: it was often used in an active and transitive sense (usually meaning either 'resurrection', the act of raising someone, or 'evacuation', the act of moving people). Its use can therefore not affect the conclusion that the resurrection of Christ is regarded, not as the natural continuation of his life in the flesh, nor as a survival of his spirit, but as an act of God.

The Bible thus confirms that from where we stand there is no road leading beyond death, that from man's point of view death must be the end. It consistently refuses to endorse the dream of religion that there must be something about us that survives. That is not its final word: it is not the message of the resurrection. But it is a word that we forget at our peril. For the resurrection of Christ is meaningful only if death is real.

Death is our end. It is a natural end. But it is more than that: it is a God-willed end. It qualifies our lives as something that God does not wish to continue for ever. It means judgment.

Many passages in the Bible hint at the connexion between sin and death, and some do more than hint (for example, Romans 5: 12-20). That does not mean that without sin man would be immortal. It is no use suggesting what would be, if only things were not as they are. The Bible is much too practical for such speculations. It is significant that the story of the fall in Genesis 3, though suggesting a connexion between sin and death, does not say that man, before the fall, was meant to be immortal. But what it does mean is that in death man comes face to face with the will of God and that, being what we are, that means judgment. The dream of immortality is not only *hybris* which will not acknowledge our human limitations but an attempt to bypass God's judgment.

It is a common error to attribute pain and sin and death to our physical nature. But if we must make the distinction between our physical and our spiritual nature, between body and soul, then it would be true to say that the ills of the body are due to its weakness, whereas those of the soul are due to its strength. It is simply not true that people sin less as they become spiritually more mature. They only sin in a different manner: the childish sins of the immature make place for the more sophisticated ones of man come of age.

Moreover, if we must make that distinction, the sins of the flesh are committed in the body but not really by the body. And frequently the body is sinned against rather than being the sinner.

But must we make that distinction at all? Is it not true to say that it is I who sin? The Bible certainly does not distinguish in that particular way. Body and soul are both words used of man in his totality. They both refer to the same man, but looked at from different angles. Sometimes the words are completely interchangeable.

The distinction made by the New Testament is that between flesh and spirit. Flesh is man as he is now, 'body and soul'. Immortality of the soul, or indeed any kind of natural immortality, would mean the endless continuation of the flesh. Such a continuation of what we are now, that would be hell: the very hell from which the death and resurrection of Christ save us.

6. RESURRECTION AND FAITH

Our conclusions so far have been negative. We have tried to place the resurrection of Christ in history, and found, not only that we have not the kind of evidence that we would require, but also that the event cannot be contained within what we mean by history. We have attempted to interpret it as an eschatological event and could not quite find room for it within the eschatological drama. We have found it unsatisfactory and misleading to speak of it as a myth. We have seen that cosmological problems may affect the presentation but have no bearing on the message itself. And we have finally found that it would be erroneous to connect the resurrection of Christ with a continued existence of the personality.

Where does that leave us? At a dead end? In a sense, yes. Death is the end of our road and it is no use trying to probe beyond. Human searching, if it is really honest, sincere and critical, can only end in a profound agnosticism. There is no way from us to God.

If the risen Christ lives in the manner of God, then what is true of any attempts to prove the existence of God, also holds good of any attempts to define the resurrection of Christ in terms of the phenomenal world. The arguments put forth from time to time to demonstrate the 'existence' of God have always sounded pretty impressive to the faithful but have notably failed to convince those who needed convincing.

Either God is, or he is not. But, whatever the truth, no argument, no reasoning, no research, no experiment will reach him, or he would not be God. Either Christ was raised from the dead, or he was not. But no argument, no reasoning, no research, no experiment will bring the truth to light, or he would not be the risen Lord. Either he is beyond human searching, or he would be a mere resuscitated corpse, and that would be the very opposite of the living Lord.

Yet there were those who saw him who cannot be seen, there are those who met him who cannot be found and knew him who cannot be known. That is what we call faith.

The word 'faith' is often used in a general sense, meaning religion. But that is a careless and even mistaken use of the word. We are using it here in a narrower, more precise and more pregnant sense. In this sense faith is found only in some few religions, not at all in primitive and antique religions but only in the Israelite-Christian-Moslem world. There are indeed some parallels, among others in Hinduism and in Mahayana Buddhism, but even they are not particularly close. Faith is really something quite unique; and to those who know it, it is not a religious phenomenon but a gift of God.[1]

The latter is, of course, already a conclusion drawn by the faith itself. But, though faith is always *our* faith, something that *we* do, there is no human accounting for it. It cannot be achieved as the result of hard work, or as the outcome of much study, or research, or experiment, not even by meditation. There is no human standpoint from where we can view God.

Consequently there is no way of demonstrating that faith is a gift of God. Though there is no human way of accounting for it, regarding it as a gift of God is itself a decision of faith. It has sometimes been called a leap in the dark.[2] That such a leap in the dark is a risk worth taking can only be found out by actually doing it.

The search for the living God cannot start until the faith is already there. '*Nemo te quaerere valet, nisi qui prius invenerit*', 'no one is able to seek thee but he who has already found'.[3] Faith is the attitude of the man who seeks God because God has sought him. Faith is primarily God's business, and ours only in second place.[4] Therefore God is not, strictly speaking, the object, but the subject of faith.

Both the Hebrew[5] and Greek[6] words usually rendered 'faith' refer to the object rather than the subject of the act of believing: they want to say something about him whom one believes in rather than about him who believes.[7] Outside the Bible the Greek word is normally translated 'fidelity', 'faithfulness', 'reliability'. It is not so much the confidence one has in a person as the ground for that confidence. It is the firm foundation on which such confidence rests. The same, up to a point, is true of non-religious usage in English. If I say that I have faith in a person, I do not really want to say something about myself but about that other person: I mean that he is the kind of person one can rely on.

A 'firm foundation' would, indeed, be a good translation of the words we are discussing. If someone has faith in God, or faith in Christ, it means that he has a firm foundation, not in himself but in God or in Christ. In the final resort it is a statement about God rather than about the believer.

The paradox of faith is that, though it is God's gift, it is at the same time the act of believing, and as such an act of man. It is not a religious *habitus*, nor is it something that one can possess (the expression, 'to have faith', is really not very exact): it is realized only in the act of believing. And believing is something that can only be done freely. In fact, this is what faith and agnosticism have in common, and what distinguishes them both from religion: they are both free decisions. Regardless of the origin of the word,[8] religion always means that one is not free. One might indeed say that the gift of faith consists in the freedom to choose for God.

Both faith and agnosticism can be experienced as a great liberation, and therefore as a great joy. It is surely not by accident that Sartre has expressed this sense of liberation, of being free from religion, in exactly the same words which Pascal used to express his joy at meeting the living God, '*Joie, joie, pleurs de joie*', 'Joy, joy, tears of joy'.[9]

To believe, or not to believe, that is a decision which is not the result of careful examination of the evidence. It is a primary decision which precedes any such examination. Call it an axiom, if you like; but it is not even the first link in a chain of argument. It is an existential decision, freely made.

That has important consequences. It means that all apologetics are in vain. They can bolster up the faith of those who already believe (though it must be doubted if their faith, which is, after all, God's gift, really needs such support). However much the believer may find his faith sup-

ported by the experience of life, or by an intelligent, rational
and reasonable exposition of what he believes, those are not
the foundations on which his faith rests. Psychologically he
may perhaps feel the need of some defence before the tribunal
of reason. Or he may feel the need of some support in his
own experience. It is not always easy to be entirely helpless.
But ultimately the free act of faith rests in the living God
himself.

It also means that there is no method by which one can
impart faith to another person. Every conversion naturally
has a psychological side also, and there is no reason why one
should not use the best possible methods to present the
gospel. But even the best method could not be more than the
instrument through which the gospel is proclaimed. One
ought therefore to be extremely careful with high-pressure
methods of evangelism. Once the stage is reached where
people are no longer really free, where they have been so
manipulated that their minds are no longer their own, they
have been robbed of what belongs to the essence of the faith.
Whatever results such methods may have, brainwashing can
scarcely be regarded as a means of setting people free.
Admittedly God, in his freedom, can undo the harm we have
done. And sometimes, after having been initially stampeded
into some kind of Christian religion, people do ultimately
still find true freedom in Christ. But that is another matter
altogether, and God's freedom should not be used as an excuse for our misdemeanour.

It would have saved many sincere Christians a lot of
heartbreak if they had not expected new methods to win the
world for Christ, but had realized that faith is not theirs but
God's to give. Our task is to present Christ to the world, but
God alone can set men free to believe.

And finally it means that within the phenomenal world
the resurrection of Christ has no visible extension beyond
the faith and obedience of those who believe. That does not
mean that the resurrection of Christ has no reality outside
that faith, or that it is identical with the belief in the resur-

rection. But it does mean that the faith of the believers is the only manner in which the risen Christ appears on the level of phenomenal existence.

That does not make the Christian faith irrational. If it did, all knowledge would be irrational. For there is no knowledge that does not rest ultimately on some axiom. Indeed, all human life would then be irrational. For in the last resort, however much we may rationalize our decisions afterwards, the fundamental decisions are of an existential nature. That 'the heart has its reasons of which reason knows nothing'[10] is true, not only of those who do, but also of those who do not put their trust in Christ.

7. CONCLUSION

The resurrection of Christ is known only to the Christian faith, which itself is not a human quality or achievement or indeed a religious phenomenon, but cannot be accounted for other than as a gift of God. There is no way of defining the resurrection of Christ within the categories of human knowledge. Saying that this should be obvious, as 'one cannot put a quart into a pint pot', would be vastly understating the fundamental qualitative distinction between the reality of God and the phenomenal world.[1]

Consequently anything one can say about the resurrection of Christ will have to be rooted in the faith in the risen Lord. If this meets with the criticism that it implies a predisposition in favour of faith, the obvious reply is that any other approach conceals a predisposition in favour of unbelief.[2] In relation to God there is no such thing as neutrality.

3

THE MESSAGE OF THE RESURRECTION

I. THE RISEN LORD RESTORES THE RELATIONSHIP

Any discussion of the resurrection of Christ which is not based on the faith in the risen Lord is a blind-alley: it could not have the risen Christ for its subject. We shall therefore have to turn to the testimony of those who saw him who cannot be seen.

The first witnesses were people who had met Jesus and put their trust in him. This trust was probably largely undefined, it was connected with a living person rather than any views about that person. At a later date they would say that in some way in him they had been confronted with God, and refer to him as the Son of God.

It seems pretty certain that Jesus did not refer to himself as the Son of God,[1] and it is doubtful if the disciples ever, while he was in the flesh, thought of Jesus other than as a man. The Gospels make it clear that they connected him with certain eschatological expectations, but these expectations varied, and in any case did not imply any Christology, any doctrine of the nature of the Messiah. The idea that Jesus was in any way divine, let alone that he was God, would not for one moment have suggested itself to them.

In the teaching of Jesus himself the emphasis was on the kingdom of God. We have already had occasion to refer to this (page 57). It was one line of eschatological expectation: the expectation that God, in his own good time, 'in the latter days', would establish his just and righteous government on earth. How this is to come about is a matter on which the relevant literature is far from unanimous. Apocalyptic writings, though they rarely use the expression 'the kingdom of God',[2] describe the inauguration of the age to come as a great cosmic event.[3] Since the pioneer work of Weiss and Schweitzer this is generally regarded as the background of the New Testament message of the kingdom of God.

However, in the rabbinic literature the term 'the kingdom of God', or, more frequently, 'the kingdom of heaven', usually refers to God's eternal sovereignty, then also to his special relationship with Israel, and, connected with the latter, to the individual's acknowledgement of God's rule.[4] 'Taking upon oneself the yoke of the Kingdom', is used specifically of the recitation of the Shema (Deuteronomy 6: 4, etc.), but also of obedience unto death. Even when the rabbinic sources refer to the Kingdom as something in the future, when they speak of the coming messianic kingdom, the term is not eschatological in the strict sense of the word: the Kingdom is something in history. The Zealot movement had obvious connexions with that.

Notwithstanding the rabbinic use and the *a priori* likelihood that Jesus would have emulated that use, it is widely taken for granted that his message of the Kingdom refers to the eschatological expectation of a cosmic catastrophe.[5] If so, he has made drastic changes and reductions.[6] For it seems that in the preaching of Jesus the kingdom of God, at least for the present, has no extension beyond the obedience of those who hear his voice and heed his commands. That appears to link his message with the rabbinic, non-apocalyptic, use of the term rather than with Jewish apocalyptics. It seems to indicate that our Lord did not primarily have the apocalyptic use of the term in mind. The proclamation of the kingdom of God is a call to obedience.

As we saw before (page 57) that is entirely in keeping with the Old Testament use of the title 'King' for YHVH. To Jesus the kingdom of God is a present reality, it is present here and now, it is 'in the midst of you' (Luke 17: 21).[7] If one wants to call that 'realized eschatology',[8] then it must be only with a very unusual interpretation of what constitutes 'eschatology'. Jesus seems to be speaking of the Kingly rule exercised through him here and now, present in him in such a way that it can in every way be entirely identified with him: he is the *autobasileia*.

But that does mean that his coming is a decisive event, *the* decisive event, and that the confrontation with him is a critical moment, the moment of decision. In that confrontation it is decided on whose side we are, whether we acknowledge the sovereignty of God or whether we do not. It is a decision which is ultimately in God's hands, but even so it is one that becomes real only in the decision which we make. The presence of Jesus Christ is therefore the *eschaton* in a far more radical sense than any cosmic drama could ever be.

The other line of eschatology, the expectation of the Messiah, seems to have been no part of the teaching of Jesus. As far as we know he never referred to himself as the Messiah. On one or two occasions, when others applied the title to him he does not seem to have contradicted. But that is the most one can say, and it is something entirely different from calling himself the Messiah. That may be connected with the widespread expectation of the Messiah as a political and military hero, which was certainly not the role he wished to play. The argument has sometimes been overstated. We have no evidence that our Lord dissociated himself completely from the national hopes of his people. But his own particular calling did not lie in that field. He had another task to do, and the use of the title 'Messiah' could only have been misleading.

It must be added that he did not claim any divine honour for himself. The Gospel according to John seems to dispute that statement, but two points ought to be taken into account. In the Gospel according to John we are confronted with the risen Lord interpreting what he had said in the days of his flesh (see page 51). And moreover even in John's

Gospel the Lord's claims are largely only implicit and rarely stated explicitly. In the other Gospels sayings in which his claims are clearly implied are rare, though not entirely absent. And on one occasion Jesus emphatically disclaims divine honour (Mark 10: 18).

Yet he spoke with authority, not the borrowed authority of the scribes, but as one having his own authority (Mark 1: 22), an authority which needed no credentials. The assertion that when he has spoken there is no room for contradiction (Matthew 5: 22, and elsewhere) speaks for itself. Also the manner in which he called people to follow him, and gathered his disciples, not around a new teaching but around his person, seems strange behaviour for a man who makes no claims for himself.

His disciples were drawn, not by any claims he made for himself, nor by the actual content of his teaching, nor by any ideas they had about him, but simply by him as a person. Even so, even though they were not consciously aware of why this should be so, it seems clear that in him they knew themselves to be confronted with God, that God acted and spoke through him, that, as it was said afterwards in retrospect, he was 'the Word of God' (John 1: 1).

That does not detract from the fact that the disciples did have some expectations connected with Jesus. It is now no longer possible to pinpoint those expectations exactly. The Gospels were written when the story of his death and resurrection were part of the Christian message, and any ideas the disciples had before those events were completely irrelevant. But the Gospels make it abundantly clear that the catastrophe of the cross shocked them profoundly. The Gospels, it is true, also tell us that Jesus had foretold his death and resurrection, but add that the disciples had not understood him. The latter is often regarded as a reason to doubt that Jesus actually did foretell his death and resurrection. But surely their not understanding is hardly surprising. Precisely because their hopes were based on their relationship with Jesus, a relationship with a person, they now found themselves without any hope in the world, without any future.

Then the risen Lord appears to them. Their first reaction is fear. Luke tells us they thought he must be a *pneuma*, a ghost from the realm of the dead. One wonders if Luke, being a Greek, realized the implications of that: he makes a point of telling us that a ghost has not flesh and bones like Jesus had (Luke 24: 39). But the real point about those in Sheol is not that they are disembodied but that they are dead. And the great thing about the risen Lord is precisely that he is not dead but alive.

Luke does, however, quote the important words, 'that it is I myself' (Luke 24: 39). The heart of the matter is the recognition of the Lord, who died and is alive.

That recognition is an important aspect, one might say, *the* important aspect, of the resurrection stories. We find it at the end of the story of the men on the road to Emmaus (Luke 24: 31), in the appearance in the upper room (Luke 24: 39), in the appearance to Mary Magdalene (John 20: 16), to the disciples without Thomas (John 20: 20) and with Thomas (20: 27), and in the appearance by the lakeside (John 21: 7). It is not mentioned in the two Matthew Christophanies (Matthew 28: 9, 17-18) but these seem to be the exceptions.

In the appearance to Saul on the road to Damascus there can, of course, be no recognition. Even so, if we can rely on Luke's testimony, the Lord's identity is the important point (Acts 9: 5; 22: 8; 26: 15). Just as Thomas, when he expresses his doubts, does not want proof that what the others have seen is not imaginary, but wants to identify the Lord, so Paul also wants to know who it is who has appeared to him. The real question is therefore, not, *what* has appeared, but *who* has appeared.

Faith in the resurrection of Christ is faith in the living Lord: a relationship with a living person. It is not so much a belief about him as a tie with him. And to the first believers the resurrection was the restoration of that fellowship they had had with him before his crucifixion. The manner of his presence among them was different but it was real, and he was still the same Lord.

We saw that their faith in him before his death was not expressed in dogmatic terms. If they called him 'the Son of God' that did not imply any Christology, any particular doctrine about his nature. Their faith was a personal relationship with someone they trusted, someone on whom they depended, someone from whom they expected they knew not what. It was a relationship with someone of flesh and blood who had walked among them, whose companions they had been, whose meals they had shared, and whom they had seen in action. They had seen his concern for others: note how often we read that Jesus saw a person, implying that that seeing of his must have been something quite out of the ordinary.[9] They had been able to observe how he served without any strings attached: when Jesus served he did not ask for anything in return; those whom he healed were not usually asked to follow him. His life was truly a life for others: he was 'the man for others'.[10] They had also witnessed his extraordinary authority and seen how a confrontation with Jesus produced a parting of the ways according to whether the challenge of that confrontation was or was not accepted. But they did not just know much about him. *They knew him.*

That faith had been badly shaken by his death. Of any convictions they may have had about him there was not much left. They were still attached to him, very much so in fact. But he was dead and gone, and that was the end of him.

But the risen Lord restores the fellowship. He does that by extending to Peter the privilege of a new calling (John 21: 15-19), by calling Mary Magdalene by name (John 20: 16), by conversations with some of the disciples (Luke 24: 13-27, and elsewhere), and especially by eating with them (Luke 24: 28-35, 41-43; John 21: 9-14; Acts 10: 40-41).

Luke's rather massive description of the latter (24: 41-43) has sometimes given rise to fanciful speculations on the physical nature of the Lord's risen body. No doubt this was part of what Luke had in mind, perhaps in an attempt to contradict any 'spiritualist' interpretation of the resurrection.

But the real point is something else. A meal establishes the closest fellowship between people. One does not really know a person until one has had a meal or at least a drink with him. There is something about eating and drinking together that uniquely unites people. It is not surprising that meals play a large part in religious worship. But even an ordinary 'secular' meal is a sacred occasion. In the East it is still true today that a guest, once he has accepted the hospitality of a meal, is sacrosanct: he belongs to the community and enjoys its fellowship and its protection. At those meals where the risen Lord revealed himself to the disciples their fellowship with the Lord was restored in the fullest sense.

It is of little consequence whether the disciples, after the death of Jesus, continued to meet as they had done before his death (at a meal), and the Lord appeared on those occasions, or whether the appearances of the risen Lord gave rise to the common meals. What matters is that the risen Lord, especially at meals, restored his fellowship with the disciples.

This is of the utmost importance for the character of the Christian faith. Because Christians, in order to speak of their faith, have to define the message in the form of propositions, in other words have to formulate some kind of doctrine, one is inclined to identify the doctrine with the faith proper. But the faith proper is not the acceptance of the doctrine, not the assent to certain propositions, but an I-Thou relationship with a living Lord. Doctrine is extremely important. It formulates the implications of this relationship. But the acceptance of any Christian doctrine, even were it the most correct doctrine, is not by itself evidence of a living faith, let

alone identical with that faith. The faith is different in kind.
No doubt the Church has to watch over the presentation of
her message and to guard against misrepresentation of the
gospel. In order to do that she has to take her doctrine
seriously. But the faith itself is not the acceptance of certain
propositions but the encounter with a person, the encounter
with Jesus Christ.

Things and persons can be to us either 'it' or 'he' or 'she',
or they can be 'thou':[11] we can either experience, observe,
describe and use them, or we can encounter them as a living
'thou'. The phenomenal world is usually treated in the first
manner. Even people are not always really met, really en-
countered. They are observed, treated, used or dealt with,
according to circumstances. Now and then, however, we see
a person not with our eyes but with our heart, we really do
encounter him. We enter, perhaps only for a brief moment,
into an I-thou relationship.

That is what happened when Jesus accepted his disciples
into his fellowship, that is what happened when the risen
Lord appeared to his disciples and ate with them. And that
happens today when people not merely believe that Jesus
Christ was raised from the dead but encounter the living
Lord. It goes without saying that this is not to be understood in an emotional sense. It is not the mere experience of
the risen Lord we are speaking about. Experience still
belongs to the it-world. We are speaking of that unique non-
phenomenal event called faith, in which the Lord presents
himself.

2. GOD WAS IN CHRIST

Faith in Jesus Christ is a relationship with him. This relationship can exist while the believer has no idea at all of its
implications. Nevertheless the relationship with Christ does
imply certain things about him. The *fides qua creditur*, the
faith by which one believes, the relationship with the living
Lord, is the faith proper, but, if one wants to speak about it

at all, the *fides quae creditur*, the faith which is believed, the content of what one believes about Christ, is of the utmost importance.

The appearances of the risen Lord restored the relationship of Christ with his disciples. They also confirmed that their faith in him had been justified. In this connexion F. W. A. Korff speaks of a rehabilitation of the Crucified.[1] That, needless to say, is not meant to suggest a public demonstration of any kind. The Lord did not appear to all and sundry, and certainly not to those who crucified him. Yet Korff speaks of a rehabilitation before the world. Some caution is needed here. The world has carried on after the resurrection very much as it did before. In the phenomenal world the resurrection of Christ has not become apparent other than in the faith of the believers. That faith is its only visible extension in the world. Christ does precisely not show himself before the world in any other way.

This much is true, that the disciples' faith in the Lord had been badly shocked by his crucifixion, and that the appearances of the risen Lord restored their faith in Christ. But that is something entirely different from a rehabilitation before the world.

One might argue that their faith should not have needed that.[2] But it is very little use saying what should have been. Subjectively the disciples did need this confirmation that their faith in Christ had been justified.[3] No argument as to what their faith ought to have been like can alter the fact that they needed this. Without this confirmation neither they nor we would have known that the Lord is alive, and that God was in Christ. One might indeed say that the 'forty days' of the appearances are the time of God's revelation *par excellence*.[4]

That God was in Christ is the heart of the Christian message. It is also the most difficult thing to put into words, such words as may give us some understanding of what we are talking about. Both those who hold to some concept, any concept, of God, and those who regard any such concept as impossible as well as irrelevant, are bound to meet almost insuperable difficulties when faced with this message.

These difficulties have presented themselves in a variety of forms. At the moment they seem to be expressed in the 'death of God' controversy. The great value of this controversy is that it pinpoints the impossibility of connecting the message concerning Christ with any god who is a postulate of human religion or merely an answer to human needs.

There are two reasons why the question did not present itself to the New Testament authors in quite the same way. The obvious one is, of course, that they believed in the reality of God, whereas many today do not. But much more important is this: the God of Israel is precisely not a postulate of human religion. One of the striking features of the Old Testament is the relative absence of metaphysics.[5] The living God is always the One who speaks and who is known only through his word and his acts. It is his word that is heard and known, and, in faith, trusted and obeyed. This God is never to be found at the end of a road of human thought, human religion, or human effort. It is significant that, if there is a Hebrew word for 'religion', it must be one of the best guarded secrets of all time: it is certainly never used in the Old Testament. God is simply the One who speaks, the One who is present in his word (or absent in his silence, 1 Samuel 3: 1). It is advisable to keep that in mind when the New Testament authors refer to 'God'.

We have seen (page 83) that, during Christ's life on earth, the disciples had no formula to describe how God was in Christ. They had no 'Christology'. There is a paradox in their attitude to Jesus. On the one hand they shared with him his wanderings through the country, had their meals with him, and in every respect shared a common life with him. There is no evidence that they regarded him as other than a man, and to call him 'God' would probably have appeared blasphemous to them. On the other hand there is much evidence that they trusted him in a manner in which God alone can be trusted, that they obeyed him as one should obey

God alone. The few occasions when they questioned his words seem to confirm rather than contradict this (for example, Mark 8: 32).

But there is more. When Jesus proclaims the forgiveness of sins it is obvious that this is God's forgiveness. Yet he seems to do this by his own authority. A good illustration is Mark 2: 1-12. The point of the controversy is the Lord's authority to forgive sins. His saying, 'My son, your sins are forgiven', need not have meant other than, 'God has forgiven your sins'. Only by implication can it be understood as referring to his own authority. Yet both his followers and his adversaries take it for granted that he does act and speak by his own authority. The scribes knew very well that God forgives sins. That was not the issue. The issue was that Jesus, though never making any overt claims for himself, spoke with God's own authority, and did so, evidently, quite as a matter of course.

This paradox runs through all the Gospels, though it is more obvious in Mark and John than in the others.[6] Mark emphasizes the paradox by his theology of the messianic secret. One can argue whether this theology is Mark's own creation[7] or whether it was already part of the tradition.[8] The former seems more likely. But this does not affect the conclusion that the theology of the messianic secret serves to highlight the paradox already present in the material itself: the paradox that Jesus made no claims for himself and yet that meeting him meant being confronted with God.

John seems to present a different picture. The Johannine Christ does make claims for himself. But then the Johannine Christ is the risen Lord who interprets what he said during the years of his flesh. Many interpreters complain that one can never be sure what John found in his sources and what is his own interpretation. But to John the Church's and his own interpretation were the work of the Spirit (compare John 14 26), that is, the risen Lord interpreting his own words (compare John 16: 25). Even so, most of what the Johannine

Christ says about himself is Christological only by implication.

And yet men's response to Christ is their response to God, their faith in him is faith in God, their rejection of him is their rejection of God.[9]

Christology is largely the attempt to formulate the implications of that paradox. The New Testament is not afraid to leave the paradox a paradox and the mystery a mystery. All the same, if the Christian message was to be spoken about at all, something had to be said about it. No attempt was made to solve the mystery but it had to be mentioned.

The earliest attempt to formulate the mystery is Romans 1: 3-4. On the level of the phenomenal world, 'according to the flesh', Jesus is a man, a descendant of David; but on another level, 'according to the Spirit of holiness', he is the Son of God, 'designated Son of God in power ... by his resurrection from the dead'. That can scarcely be regarded as an attempt to solve the mystery of Christ and it would be rash to interpret it in the sense of an Adoptionist Christology. Many modern interpreters are inclined to think on those lines, or at least to emphasize the temporal succession of the two modes of existence.[10] But the two statements, 'according to the flesh', and 'according to the Spirit of holiness', do not refer to the same level of reality.[11]

It is obvious, and need not be argued, that any attempt to read orthodox Christology into Paul's words is even further off the mark.

It is often maintained that the proper interpretation of the passage depends on the exact meaning of 'designated'. The Greek verb means, to 'mark off (by boundary lines)', also 'circumscribe', 'define', and 'appoint (to an office)'. The wide meaning does not allow too narrow an interpretation. The rendering 'designate' (Revised Standard Version) seems as good as any, and has the advantage that it does not burden the text with interpretations which may have been far from Paul's mind.[12] It would be too much to say that the statement of Romans 1: 3-4 is pre-theological,[13] but, though it contains the central problem of Christology, it does not provide an answer.

The title 'Son of God' does not necessarily signify the implications of the later Trinitarian and Christological dogmas. In the Old Testament the expression is used of Israel (Jeremiah 31: 20; Hosea 11: 1, and elsewhere), of the King (Psalm 2: 7, and elsewhere), and the plural can mean the people of Israel (Isaiah 43: 6, and elsewhere). Nevertheless to Paul Jesus is the Son of God in a unique sense. Though occasionally he refers to others as sons of God (Romans 8: 14, 19; 2 Corinthians 6: 18; Galatians 4: 6-7) it is clear that no one is the Son of God in the sense in which Jesus is.[14] No doubt Hellenistic influences have affected the use of the title.[15] Yet traces of the Hellenistic concept of the 'divine man' are rare and superficial. Paul's use of the title stresses that Jesus is entirely on God's side[16] but does not define how.

The title *Kyrios*, 'Lord', points in the same direction. In the Greek version of the Old Testament the title is used to render YHVH, the sacred name of the God of Israel.[17] It has been suggested that that is the origin of the New Testament use of the title for Jesus, and that the title identifies Jesus with YHVH. Others have pointed to the Hellenistic use of the word.[18] The latter seems more likely. But in either case the title claims divine honour for the *Kyrios*: he is to be worshipped. And Paul, and probably the Hellenistic Church before him, often uses the title in quotations from the Old Testament where it was a translation of YHVH, but applies the quotation to Jesus (for example, 1 Corinthians 2: 16; 2 Corinthians 3: 16; 10: 17). And sometimes it is not clear whether 'the Lord' refers to Jesus or to the Father (for example, Romans 10: 13; 1 Corinthians 3: 5; 4: 19; 2 Corinthians 5: 11). It almost seems as if Paul does not distinguish between YHVH, the Lord God of Israel, and the Lord Jesus Christ. That would be reading too much into the texts. But his use of the title does suggest that in Jesus Paul knew himself to be confronted with God.

The third title used by Paul, Christ,[19] is a rendering of the Jewish title for the Messiah, the Anointed (King). But, with the possible exception of Romans 10: 6-7, he uses the word as a proper name. In any case the title does not call for any 'Christology'.

An attempt to relate the two levels of reality is made in Philippians 2: 6-11. The passage is a hymn quoted by the author, so we need not concern ourselves with the authorship of the Epistle.[20] The hymn has the form of a myth, the myth of the descent of the Saviour.[21] But what distinguishes this myth is that on the level of phenomenal existence, during the time of his humiliation, Christ is precisely not the 'divine man': he 'emptied himself'. The *kenosis*, his emptying himself, is meant to be taken seriously. It is no mere disguise. 'The form of a servant' and 'the likeness of men' are not a mere outward appearance. It is emphasized that in human form he did not appear as a god upon earth, as the 'divine man', but 'humbled himself and became obedient unto death'. And finally we learn that after his death upon the cross God has exalted him and given him the name that is above every name, the title of *Kyrios*. The myth relates the two levels in a temporal scheme but does not answer the cardinal question of Christology: Was he then not equal with God, was he then not the *Kyrios* during the days of his humiliation?

Matthew and Luke describe the mystery in the form of the virgin birth. It is not suggested that they invented that. Both found it in their sources, though it is obvious that Luke's sources were not unanimous.[22] The Greek world was not unfamiliar with a belief in semi-divine beings with a half divine, half human parentage, and it is not surprising that the birth of Jesus was expressed in similar terms. It should be observed, though, that neither Luke nor Matthew describes the virgin birth in naturalistic terms. There is no trace of a sacred marriage between heaven and earth, between God and a mortal. The birth of Jesus is miraculous in that he has no father in the usual sense of the word, that Mary remains a virgin after the conception. It is surely significant that Matthew says that she 'was found to be with child of *the Holy Spirit*' (Matthew 1: 18), and quotes Isaiah 7: 14. That Isaiah did not speak of a virgin but of a young woman of marriageable age is irrelevant as we are not concerned with what Isaiah meant but with what Matthew wanted to convey.

To Luke the matter is complicated by the fact that his sources were not unanimous. It is clear that his sources for the opening chapters present at least two strands of tradition, one in which Joseph was regarded as the father of Jesus and one in which he was not.[23] Luke has taken considerable trouble to weld them into one consecutive narrative. The result is similar to his treatment of the resurrection stories. Luke mythologizes the incarnation as he does the resurrection.

The author who seems to come closest to an attempt at solving the mystery is the Fourth Evangelist. In the prologue to the Gospel according to John (John 1: 1-18) Jesus is identified as the *Logos*, 'the Word'.

Granted that the prologue is probably influenced by the Logos speculations of Philo,[24] and perhaps also by the Gnostic myth of redemption,[25] it would yet be unwise to overlook the function of the word of God in the Old Testament. The opening phrase, 'In the beginning was the Word', as well as the phrase, 'all things were made through him, and without him was not anything made that was made' (verse 3), recall the opening chapter of Genesis. There God creates all things by his word, that creative word that calls all things into being.[26] This same word later calls Abraham and the nation of Israel, this word calls the prophets to speak to the people. This word can also save in distress (Psalm 107: 20). And it will achieve whatever God wills (Isaiah 55: 11). In all these cases the word of God is, obviously, God speaking. Sometimes the word of God can be referred to as if it had some independent, almost personal existence (Psalm 107: 20; Isaiah 2: 1, and elsewhere).[27] But does not affect the simple fact that the word of God is God speaking.

In this sense the word of God is one of the key expressions of the Old Testament. The living God, the God of Israel, is the God who speaks, while the gods are silent.[28]

But we have to go one step further. One of the striking features of the Old Testament, as we saw (page 87), is the relative absence of metaphysics. God is simply the One who is present in his word (or absent in his silence). There is no knowledge of God other than through his word.

Whatever other influences have contributed to John's use of the term, it would seem imprudent, considering the unique importance which the Old Testament attaches to the word of God, not to take the Old Testament use of the term into consideration.[29]

If we do take this into account, then the inevitable conclusion must be that to John the Word is God speaking. Jesus, to him, is God revealing himself.

The next phrase, 'the Word was with God', personifies the Word in the manner of the Logos speculation and/or the Gnostic myth.[30] But the phrase 'the Word was God' identifies, in some sense, God with his word. The phrase is as awkward in Greek as it is in English. We can discount the translation 'the Word was a god': not only would the idea of there being a number of gods never have occurred to the author, but the phrase itself does not really allow of that interpretation. If that was what he meant he could and would have expressed himself differently. Neither does it mean 'the Word was divine'. If this is what the author meant he could have said so in perfectly good Greek without having recourse to the awkward phrase he actually did use. It could be argued that the Greek of this Gospel, though very beautiful, is not really 'good' in the strict sense of the word. That is very true, but the author does use the language confidently and competently. It seems therefore improper to assume that he meant something other than he actually wrote. We ought therefore to translate what he wrote, not what we think he ought to have written. And he wrote, 'the Word was God'.

Yet this does not seem to be an identification *tout court*. The New English Bible attempts to take that into consideration by rendering, 'and what God was, the Word was'. That translation does justice to the difficulties of the text but it still seems best to stick to the more literal rendering. If that is awkward, and difficult or even impossible to comprehend, the same holds good of the original.

The interpretation of the passage is complicated by our awareness of its connexion with the Logos speculation and the Gnostic myth. If the Gospel according to John had been produced in a vacuum, or if we were unaware of its background, we should only have to take the text itself and the Old Testament into account. Earlier exegetes were often hampered by their ignorance of the background. Our danger is that we might overlook the Old Testament connexions, that we might be so interested in the Hellenistic influences on the text that we might forget that the Old Testament has anything to do with it at all. Yet the most obvious interpretation is that God is one with his Word, thus emphasizing the reliability of the revelation in Christ. The Word is none other than God speaking. God is as good as his Word, and there is no reason to suspect that in himself God might be other than his revelation in Jesus Christ.

'And the Word became flesh.' The speaking of God is the man Jesus. The Evangelist does not operate with notions of 'divine' and 'human nature'. He speaks of God in action. No attempt is made to master the mystery of the incarnation by means of conceptual thinking.

The Church has not halted where the New Testament did. During the first three centuries we can observe the development of a number of Christologies. There is no need to discuss those here. Though they came out of the Christian Church and were therefore, in a sense, the outcome of the Church's life, they were not adopted by the Church as a whole. The Church's 'official' teaching—the expression is not actually particularly suitable—during the period confines itself to the story of the gospel.

That teaching is contained in a condensed form in the various baptismal confessions. As an example we take that of the Church at Rome, which became the basis of the later 'Apostles' Creed'. In its oldest form it probably consisted of three simple statements:

I believe in God the Father, the Ruler of all;
and in Jesus Christ his only Son, our Lord;
and in the Holy Ghost, the Holy Church, the resurrection of the body.[31]

Through the addition of details about the Lord's incarnation, life and work, this grew into a larger form:

... our Lord, who was born from the Holy Ghost and the Virgin Mary,
was crucified under Pontius Pilate and buried,
rose again from the dead on the third day,
ascended into heaven,
sits at the right hand of the Father,
from where he will come to judge the quick and the dead;

while in the third part was added, 'the forgiveness of sins'.[32]

The Eastern Church, on the whole, was more theologically minded, and there we do find phrases added which emphasize on the one hand God's work in the creation of the world, on the other hand the relation between the Father and the Son:

I believe in one God, the Father, the Ruler of all,
Maker of all things visible and invisible;

and in one Lord Jesus Christ, the only Son of God,
born from the Father before all ages,
through whom all things were made . . .

The classical dogma of the Church goes much further. The
reasons were legitimate in the circumstances. But we are
bound to misunderstand the dogma profoundly if we regard
it as an attempt to analyse God. The Trinitarian and
Christological dogmas want to ward off attempts at such
analysis which had already been made.

The doctrine of the Trinity is concerned with the relationship between the Father, the Son and the Holy Ghost. On
the one hand it seems reasonable to believe that the Son (and
the same holds good, *mutatis mutandis*, of the Holy Ghost) is
identical with the Father. But that would contradict the
gospel tradition. Unless we assume that the words in which
Jesus spoke of the Father, and especially those he spoke to
the Father, were a piece of theatre put on for the benefit of
his audience, the suggestion can be rejected out of hand. All
the same, it was, and still is, fairly widespread. It is born, no
doubt, from a very real experience that in meeting Jesus we
meet the living God. But it does not do justice to the Lord's
human life of faith and obedience. Faith in whom? Obedience to whom? And it may blind us effectively to the
challenge of his perfect and exemplary human life (see
pages 127ff).

The obvious alternative, the only alternative, is that Jesus
Christ is other than the Father, that he is either a mere
instrument of God's revelation, or a 'second god' (Arius).
One objection to that is that one cannot believe, in the full
Christian sense of the word, in more than one god. Arianism
must therefore assign a subordinate place to the Son.

More serious is that any doctrine that does not allow that
the Son is of one substance with the Father destroys the
trust in the reliability of God's revelation and indeed of God
himself. If God's Word is not God himself speaking, then
there is room left for the suspicion that God might be other

than his Word. It is easy to hold the Nicene Council up to ridicule for their bickering over one letter[33] (for that is the difference, in Greek, between 'of one substance'[34] and 'of like substance'[35]), but the one letter concerned the reliability of God's Word, and, ultimately, God's faithfulness.

The doctrine of the Trinity, that the Father, the Son and the Holy Ghost are three times the One God, rejects both possible solutions of the mystery. Due, no doubt, to the terms in which it was expressed, it has sometimes been used as if it was itself such a solution, and has, indeed, at times functioned as if it was an analysis of God.[36] The effects have been disastrous. When such a formula is regarded as an object of faith, then a formula is substituted for the living God.

But one cannot, properly speaking, believe in the Trinity, neither in the formula, nor in the Trinity as an object.[37] Christians believe in the triune God, the God and Father of our Lord Jesus Christ, whose mystery is referred to but cannot be solved in the doctrine of the Trinity. No analysis could ever have the living God for its object. God, if he is the living God, is beyond such analysis. Far from explaining the mystery, the doctrine of the Trinity leaves it a mystery and declares it inexplicable and adorable. The proper place for the Trinitarian formula is in the adoration of God.

The Christological dogma is concerned with the next question: What is the relation between the divine and human 'natures' in Christ? The notions here introduced are foreign to the Bible. The Bible does not speak in terms of divine and human 'nature'. This dogma too aims at the rejection of dangerous definitions but has left the choice of arms to the enemies.

The enemies are on the one hand a theology which keeps the two natures separate, which maintains that the divine Word of God dwelt in the man Jesus as in a temple (Nestorius), and which thus loses sight of Jesus Christ as a person, and on the other hand a theology which salvages his personality at the cost of making him a semi-divine being with one human-divine nature (Eutyches). The Councils of Ephesus and Chalcedon rejected both solutions and in fact every possible solution. The canons of Chalcedon leave the mystery a mystery: we acknowledge 'one and the same Christ . . . in two natures unconfusedly, unchangeably, indivisibly, inseparably'.[38]

It cannot be denied that the two natures have often functioned in an entirely different way. The mystery of the incarnation has often been replaced by a *concept* of the union of two natures, and that concept has been regarded as an object of faith.[39] The dogma has thus been deprived of its proper function, which is precisely to exclude the possibility of any such concept.

The classical dogma of the Church grew out of the revelation in Christ. It attempts to point out that in Christ we are meeting the living God. But it may be asked legitimately if both the Trinitarian and Christological dogmas do not seem to take the reality of God for granted and try to relate Christ to that accepted reality. In other words, whereas the road of faith leads from the known Christ to the unknown God, the dogma seems to lead from a known God to the riddle of Christ. It is our view that that is not the intention of the dogma but that it does leave itself open to such an interpretation.

This gave rise to grave problems with the increasing importance of natural theology. The beginnings of natural theology within the Church are early. But the peculiar questions it raises in connexion with Christology were not seen until much later and did not become urgent until after the Renaissance, and especially after the Enlightenment.

Natural theology claims that God is a rational postulate of human religion. It takes God for granted.[40] But as soon as God is taken for granted in this manner we start operating with a *concept* of God. For that is what a rational postulate is, a concept.

It was, of course, never suggested that God is only a concept. The concept of God was believed to be a true one, that is to say, a concept about a real God. Nevertheless, the thinking about God was conceptual thinking.

Operating with concepts of God, of divine and human natures, and, in Christology, of the union of the natures, one has to face some extremely awkward questions. For how can the divine nature take on the nature of man? Is that not a contradiction in terms?

That question, first voiced by Spinoza in the seventeenth century, dominated nineteenth-century theology. It is determined by the concept of the two natures and their relation. Within the context of that concept it is a perfectly reasonable question and, again within the context of that concept, the Church's doctrine must seem utterly unreasonable. For Jesus was a man, and, if we must operate with the concepts of human and divine natures, unless we assume that Jesus was some strange hybridic, divine-human phenomenon, neither one thing nor the other, the conclusion is inescapable that whatever differences there may have been between him and other human beings can only have been differences of degree. His may have been a greater awareness of the nearness of God, he may have been more closely in touch with God than other people and have lived his life accordingly and thereby become the greatest of God's children, but that is a matter of degree. He may have proclaimed God's will more clearly and more fully than anyone else, and thus have revealed God to us more fully and more clearly than anyone before or after him, but that would only make him the greatest of the prophets, and that again is a matter of degree.

The various types of 'modern' theology (the theology of the nineteenth century) were attempts to understand the revelation in Christ as relating to a God who was taken for granted, and within the terms of conceptual thinking. That the result was sometimes a Christianity without Christ is not surprising. But it was certainly not intended. Modern theologians were as much under his spell as their more con-

servative counterparts. Their preaching was dominated by
Christ as much as that of anyone. But to their thinking he
was a riddle.

The problem of twentieth-century theology is a different
one. We do not find it so easy to take God for granted. A
concept of God is not so self-evident as it used to be. It is perhaps characteristic of our time that God is no longer obvious.

That needs some qualification. There are many people
today, as there were before, to whom religion still means
something. But, characteristically, religious people do not
differ dramatically from others in the decisions they make
and in the manner in which they conduct their lives. Whenever important decisions are to be made it does not seem to
make much difference whether a person is a Christian or
what he is. His decisions are made without reference to his
religion. That does not mean that his religion does not give
him a great deal of support and strength and comfort when
he needs it. But it does not seem to affect his practical decisions to any great extent.

This is often attributed to the influence of Christian ethics
on the general pattern of behaviour. A large part of the
world has long been nominally Christian, and a Christian
way of life is often regarded as right even by those who are
not themselves Christians. There is a humanistic view of
what is right or wrong that is to all intents and purposes
identical with or at least indistinguishable from the Christian
ethics.

There is an element of truth in that. Naturally in a society
where, nominally at least, Christianity was dominant, it
was inevitable that many aspects of its ethics became
generally accepted. But it is not the whole truth. Humanist
ideals are not always identical with Christian ethics. They
often imply a serious criticism of Christian standards and
have sometimes been a real challenge to Christianity. Moreover the general pattern of behaviour in our modern world

is neither so Christian nor so humanistic as some would have us believe.

Furthermore, the gospel is not confined to moral precepts; neither does the Christian life coincide with living by certain rules. If Christian obedience means anything at all it is obedience to a living God. And that should be something totally different from living by certain rules or according to a code of ethics.

It is precisely in the practice of life that most people's religion is totally irrelevant and immaterial and therefore ineffective. However faithful people may be to their religion, they rarely allow their God to interfere with the business of everyday living and with their day-to-day decisions. They may live according to what they regard as his general commandments in as much as those commandments coincide with what all decent folk regard as right. But they would not dream of expecting him to make any demands beyond that, let alone contrary to that.

There is, of course, also an upsurge in cults outside mainstream religion, and many cults, religious, semi-religious, or even completely secular, cater for the needs of those 'who are made that way'. But those cults can scarcely be regarded as typical of the most advanced thinking of our time. Indeed it seems at times as if they want to avoid thinking at all costs. They are concerned, or so at least it seems, with satisfying certain needs and appealing to certain emotions. The needs and emotions are real enough. But the question of the truth about God is not asked, let alone answered.

Religion today seems to confirm rather than deny that we are without God in the world. That does not just mean that old concepts of God are no longer relevant and that we must substitute new images for old. It is something far more radical. It is this, that, wherever we seek God, we cannot find him: he just is not there. It is more than the absence of the experience of God: it is the experience of the absence of God.[41] It is what is expressed by the phrase, 'God is dead'.[42] The phrase is misleading: it sounds like a metaphysical obituary notice, which it is not. However, it expresses the very real experience that we are without God in the world.

Essentially the phrase therefore refers to the knowledge, not the reality of God. God as a necessary postulate, or a first cause, or the Master Builder of the universe, is simply unthinkable. That does not necessarily mean that he is not real. It means that he cannot be approached along the avenues of natural theology.

But when we say that God was in Christ we precisely do not mean that Christ shows us something more about someone called God, whose existence we could take for granted anyway, and about whom we could already know much even without Christ. God is the word we use for him who confronts us in Christ. And that is not, in the first instance, a metaphysical statement at all. Bonhoeffer goes as far as saying, a little paradoxically, but much to the point, '*Einen Gott, den "es gibt", gibt es nicht*', 'There is no God that "there is" '.[43]

Faith consists in putting one's trust in Jesus Christ. That can be done without any theory about him. We may well do it because in him we meet a man who is different, not in any metaphysical sense, 'because he is God' or 'the Son of God', but in that he can give real content and meaning to our lives, in that he is the One who uniquely knows the way through life and can give direction and purpose to our lives. One may well doubt if there is a living God and still regard Jesus Christ as someone who should be followed *etsi deus non daretur*, even if there was no God.[44] And that is, in fact, how some people have begun to follow Christ, thinking they were following a dead master, doubting if God could be anything like the God and Father of our Lord Jesus Christ, or even if there could be a God—only to discover somewhere along the road that Jesus Christ is very much alive and that the living God is very real.

For it is only in the practice of following Christ that one can discover that he is alive, not a dead prophet but a living Lord who is with us now, and that God is in him and that he is very much a living God. It is in the act of following Christ that one can find out that the experience of the absence of God is an illusion, very real as an experience but nevertheless an illusion.[45]

One can argue that the life of Christ would be inexplicable without the reality of the living God. That would be very true. But it would be mere theory. The real thing, the full Christian faith, the true encounter with the living God, is found only in the act of following Christ.

That means taking a chance on him. That God is at the end of the road with Christ cannot be demonstrated other than by actually walking that road. There is nothing surprising in that: it holds good of any journey. If one does not want to rely on other travellers one can only find out what is at the end of the road by making the journey—just as no British holidaymaker in France will ever know the delights of the French cuisine if he sticks to fish and chips: the proof is in the eating. And just as no amount of sex-instruction can show adequately what it is to love and be loved: that one can only know in doing.

Meeting Christ means having the opportunity of taking that chance. Whether one does take it or not is a free decision. But it is free not in the sense of a general indeterminate free will: it is a freedom which is determined by the confrontation itself, it is being persuaded by Christ himself whether he is worth taking a chance on.

The phrase 'God is dead' was first used by Nietzsche: 'God is dead. He remains dead. And we have killed him.'[46] To him the death of God is the outcome of what men have been doing.[47] More precisely it is the work of philosophers and theologians, for a god who is a concept is *per se* a dead god. The murder of God is the act by which man has made himself free—though Nietzsche knows too much about man to regard that as a cause for joy.[48] At any rate it is obvious that his phrase is not a metaphysical statement of fact but refers to a relationship: a relationship of enmity and competition.

In that light the usual arguments for or against the
Christian faith are scarcely relevant. Rational arguments
one way or the other do not really affect the decision for or
against Christ. And even the experience of the absence of
God is not decisive. Jesus Christ himself shared that experience (Mark 15: 34[49]). The decision is taken on another
level. It is an existential decision freely made (see page 75).

3. THE RISEN CHRIST: THE TRUTH ABOUT GOD

We are thus left with a certain hesitation about adopting the
Church's dogma lock, stock and barrel, while on the other
hand walking with Jesus we are left in no doubt that in him
we are confronted with the living God. And if we want to
formulate that more closely it will not be easy to improve on
the Trinitarian and Christological dogmas: that the Father,
the Son and the Holy Ghost are three times the one God;
that Jesus Christ is real man and true God. One may perhaps
wonder if it is really necessary to attempt such closer formulation, but if one attempts it at all one will find that nothing
other than the classic dogma will do.

Either way, with or without such closer formulation,
speaking of God is of necessity speaking of his revelation,
that is to say, speaking of Christ. Such speaking of Christ
does not necessarily lead to a minimum theology. How all-
embracing such a Christomaniac theology can be is demonstrated for instance, if demonstration is wanted, by Karl
Barth's *Church Dogmatics*.

It cannot, of course, be the intention of the present work
to provide a manual of Christian doctrine or even a minimum theology. But we must draw a few lines which follow
from the confrontation with the risen Christ, lines which, we
believe, any theology disregards at its peril.

The resurrection of Christ relates the earthly life of Jesus to
its origin in God.[1] That earthly life is what we know about
Jesus Christ, and it is there that we can find what God is like.

However, we ought to be careful. Jesus was not *the* ideal man but a concrete man, with the individual characteristics which distinguish one man from another. We have no information about those at all. We do not know the colour of his hair or his eyes, whether he was short or tall, nor do we know what his character was like. We cannot tell whether the Gospels refrain on purpose from giving us that kind of picture. We can only state the fact that we are singularly uninformed about 'Jesus according to the flesh' (2 Corinthians 5: 16: one is tempted to translate, 'the psychology of Jesus'; that would be too modern, though it comes as close to the author's intention as one can get; the Revised Standard Version and the New English Bible miss the point). We only know about his work: his words, deeds, passion and resurrection. It is really amazing how much we do not know about him. For instance, we are not even told whether or not he was married,[2] though it is usually taken for granted that he was not. Like everybody else's his life was bound to be full of incidental peculiarities. But we are told of those only in so far as they were relevant to his proper task.

Secondly, his words and actions did not show the truth about God in the abstract. Through his life and work, through his words and actions, his passion and resurrection, God spoke to us and acted for us, but always in concrete situations. There can be no doubt that God gives himself as he is, that he is true in revealing himself, that we can rely on him as he reveals himself in Jesus Christ. But that knowledge of God is practical and comes from the actual confrontation with his word and work in Jesus Christ.

In Christ God reveals his love towards us. The love of God towards men is that he desires and has fellowship with them. We believe that God knows and loves with his heart, that his love is not a piece of play-acting. Nevertheless we cannot speak of the love of God other than as it is revealed in action, in the life and death and resurrection of our Lord Jesus Christ.

In his earthly life the Lord shares the lives of people and makes them share his. He does not love from a distance or from above, he does not patronize people, he stands where they stand, he is one of them. And he is inescapably so. He is not like those who want to know how the other half lives and share their lives for a while but always with the knowledge that they can escape. He shares our lives from birth to death with no escape.

It is precisely this that makes it so difficult for us to think of him as presenting God: that he stood where we stand, that he became one of us in every respect. In his earthly life he was subject to the ordinary human limitations. Even his miracles, though regarded as signs of extraordinary power, do not exceed the limits of what was regarded as humanly possible. And they are never demonstrations of what he can do: they always respond to a human need. That holds good even of the Gospel according to John, though that Gospel tends to emphasize more than the others their character as 'signs'. The only exception, the cursing of the fig tree (Mark 11: 12-14, 20-21), probably grew out of a parable; but even in its present form the Evangelist takes some pains to connect it with what every man can do if he has faith (Mark 11: 22-26).

Jesus' human limitations play an important part in the story of the temptation (Matthew 4: 1-11; Luke 4: 1-13). Both the temptation to turn stones into bread and to throw himself from the pinnacle of the Temple are temptations to claim an exceptional position for himself, temptations to expect that he would not be subject to the same limitations as other people. Surely if Jesus is the Son of God he should not be expected to go without food when he is hungry: God can make bread. Surely if he is the Son of God he cannot drop dead like other people: God will protect him.

The same limitations provoke some mockery when he is dying on the cross. Surely if Jesus is the Son of God he does not have to suffer the same as other people (Mark 15: 29-31; Luke 23: 37, 39).

But Jesus had to be tempted and to suffer the same as other people, even though both his temptations and his passion are related to his peculiar situation. But then everyone is tempted according to his character and situation, and everyone suffers according to his own peculiar circumstances. The love of Christ is no distant benevolence: he stood where we stand.

Secondly, the Lord sees the real needs of people, not only their spiritual needs but the needs of their bodies, even the apparently most trivial needs. Many people have taken offence at the story of the wedding at Cana (John 2: 1-11). The whole thing seems so trivial and unnecessary. But the Evangelist calls it the first of the Lord's signs, and he means more than that it is the first in time.[3] It is the principal of his signs in that it shows right at the outset what Christ is really like. When confronted with the ordinary, quite mundane needs of ordinary people he is concerned and deals with them. We need not concern ourselves with the questions which have occupied so many minds, as, for instance, whether perhaps the miracle story grew out of one in which the wine was produced in a perfectly natural manner. It is much more important that we should see our Lord joining people in their ordinary pleasures and seeing to it that the fun of the party is not spoiled.

Also, he always seems to have time for people. A good example is the blessing of the children (Mark 10: 13-16). Children cannot do anything for the kingdom of God. And the Master is busy. So we can understand the disciples regarding them as a nuisance and trying to keep them away. But Jesus has time for them, as he has for Bartimaeus (Mark 10: 46-52) and for the woman with the flow of blood (Mark 5: 25-31), as he has time for the men on the road to Emmaus (Luke 24: 13-32), for Mary Magdalene (John 20: 11-17), for Thomas (John 20: 26-29), for Peter (John 21: 15-23), and for countless others since.

He also has time for people in another sense. When we say that we have no time for a person, we often mean that we do not think much of him, that we do not regard him as worthy of our time and effort, that we cannot be bothered with him. Jesus had time for the poor, the sick and the lonely, but also for the outcast and the wicked, for those whom others might regard as beyond praying for. He welcomed sinners and ate with them (Mark 2: 13-17; Matthew 11: 19; Luke 15: 2). He was a friend of tax collectors (collaborators with the Roman enemy) and other bad characters (Matthew 11: 19). He extended the hand of fellowship to those who regarded themselves as far from the kingdom of God and drew them into the fellowship of his love.

The picture which the Gospels give us of the band of disciples is one of a happy family where people belong together with each other and with the Master, not because they are such excellent people or because they deserve that kind of fellowship but simply because he wants their company. There is, of course, the exception of Judas but the horror with which his betrayal is referred to shows how much it was regarded as an offence against a most intimate and sacred fellowship and togetherness. The word 'family' is really a most suitable description. In a good family you are accepted, you are loved, simply because you belong to the family. You do not have to do anything in particular to get accepted, even though you are expected to do your part. You do not have to prove yourself. You just belong. When Christ spoke of God as the Father he was not only emphasizing something that had always been part of the faith of Israel. That too, of course. But in his own dealing with people he acted on family lines. The fatherhood of God is not merely a piece of his teaching: it is God's love in action.

That love is shown at its deepest level in his ability and willingness to suffer, not only with us, but for us. The cross of Christ is what happens when men are confronted with God. The Lord was crucified not through some strange turn of destiny, nor was he murdered at the hands of some extraordinary monsters of iniquity: he was led to his death by quite commonplace people very much like ourselves, not without some malice, not without some wresting of the law, but not more than is frequently the case in human relations and behaviour. He was crucified because people were what they were, and that means ultimately because we are what we are.

It has recently been suggested that Jesus had been involved in some rebellion against the Romans and therefore condemned to death. There is not a scrap of evidence to support that suggestion. This much is true, that his attitude to the national hopes of his people was not so negative as some would have us believe. Also that Pilate's part in the crucifixion was more serious than is generally assumed.[4] But nowhere in any reliable source do we find a hint that he was involved in armed resistance. He was crucified simply because people are what they are, because we are what we are.

The resurrection shows that in laying hands on Jesus men aimed at God. The cross is the crowning event of our rebellion against God: 'We do not want this man to reign over us' (Luke 19: 14: the reference is clearly to the trial before Pilate).

We are not suggesting that Caiaphas, Pilate and company were aware of that. Of course they were not. They were merely protecting the existing political and religious fabric of society. They might have been dealing with anyone. But in dealing with just anyone they were in fact attacking God. That is the disastrous fatality of the human condition, that our normal aggressiveness aims at the living God. Only in the case of Jesus it hit the target. Naturally the outcome of the conflict cannot be doubted. The attack on God is not only sinful but quite ludicrous. How can we hope to get away with it?

Yet the outcome is not the ruin of man but the death of the Son of God. No one saves him from his death at the hands of men, no disaster befalls Caiaphas or Pilate. Jesus dies like everyone else. That is how far God has identified himself with us. That is how far he will go in what he is prepared to suffer at our hands. That is love at its most perfect: the willingness to suffer at the hands of the beloved.

When the risen Lord appeared to his disciples that fellowship of love was renewed. The renewal is described most vividly in the conversation between the Lord and Peter (John 21: 15-19). To Peter, before he met the risen Lord, Jesus was not only dead and gone, but Peter himself, through his denial (Mark 14: 11-72; John 18: 17, 25-27), had severed himself from his dead Lord. The risen Lord does not shower his unfaithful disciple with reproaches: he just reminds him that he belongs to the family and that the old promises and commands still hold good: 'Simon, son of John, do you love me? . . . Tend my sheep'.[5] There is no demand of a preceding act of penitence, just the outstretched hand of the love of Christ.

And this is what we still find when we meet Christ: the outstretched hand of his love. Here is someone who knows all about us and still accepts us. Here is someone before whom we do not have to pretend. Here is someone who takes us where he finds us and takes us just the way we are.

That love is revealed to us as God's *grace*: it is unmerited love, his undeserved favour towards us.[6] God's dealing with us is always a work of his grace. The creation and the gift of life are already gifts of his grace, unmerited, undeserved. God was under no obligation to create us and to give life. But when we speak of God's grace we imply not only that we are not worthy but that we are unworthy. The cross shows how unworthy. The cross, after all, was not a mere incident: it was the outcome of what people are, that is to say, what we are. We are not just undeserving, we are rebels. God's grace overcomes that rebellion. We kill God-with-us on Good Friday, but on Easter Day his love has the last word.

The resurrection of Christ is indeed a criticism of what we are and do. But it is a criticism that is given without reproach. Grace implies a particular kind of humour. It is noteworthy that the Hebrew word for 'grace'[7] is also used in a secular sense for a certain brand of humour.[8] It is the kindly, but costly, humour that has known much pain but overcomes in the end with a smile. That kind of humour is implied when we speak of the grace of God. It is the sunny atmosphere which we find in the Easter message if we can learn to discard the dark spectacles of our solemnity.

God's grace means that in our relationship with him everything depends on him and nothing on us, that God is on our side even if we are not on his, that God is with us even if we are without him or even against him.

We depend on God, on his free grace in Jesus Christ. His grace is free. But that does not mean that he could be gracious but also withhold his favour. In a sense it may be true to say that he is free to act one way or another. But his grace is not incidental, not one side of his character against which other sides must be balanced. If we can rely at all on God as he has revealed himself in Jesus Christ, then God's grace is none other than God himself in his undeserved love for us, then God is not merely gracious, he is grace as he is love. In his grace we have God himself, his very heart, the whole of God. In his grace God gives himself as he is. He regards us as precious because he sees with his heart and not with his eyes (see page 176, note 9).

In the resurrection of Christ God reveals to us the *holiness* of his love. In that it is distinguished from all other love. That holiness is not a definition and limitation of his love. It rather means that even in his love, even in his giving himself to us he remains the Lord. Indeed, precisely in his giving himself he remains himself, he remains the Lord. In the sacrifice on the cross and the victory of the resurrection God maintains his sovereignty, that is, the sovereignty of his grace, against all enmity and opposition. That is what happened on the cross, when no enmity could change his love for those who had rejected him. That is what happened in the resurrection when Jesus Christ was victorious over sin and death and over those who had crucified him. The resur-

rection unmasks the righteousness and wisdom and religion
of man and shows them up for what they are: they are the
things that made man crucify the Lord of life. But precisely
in that *démasqué* their fascination and power are cancelled,
and we are set free to live by the grace of God, no longer
dependent on our own righteousness, wisdom and religion,
but on God's grace alone.

The love of God is *mercy and compassion*. We have seen how the
life and the cross of Jesus are full of compassion, a sharing of
our lives and deaths. It may be true that man's plight is tied
up with his guilt, that he has chosen his own desires, his own
will, his own presumed liberty, his own gods whom he will
serve. But it is also true that his presumption is pitiful folly,
his abused liberty hard servitude, his desire and lust bitter
pain. The wonder of God's mercy is that he is more concerned with our plight than with our guilt. He is merciful and
stands by us in our condition, indeed makes our condition
his own. He takes our sin into his own heart and removes its
sting from our hearts.

One constant source of conflict between Jesus and the
scribes was his refusal to segregate himself from the wicked.
He presents God not as standing over against the sinner but
by his side. He identifies himself with man, not in the abstract, with the ideal man, but with people as they actually
are, in their sins. He even refuses to be called good (Mark 10:
18).

In Jesus Christ God makes our plight his own. On the
cross that was true but hidden. Through the resurrection we
know, truly, *he* has borne our griefs and carried our sorrows.
Thus he shows his mercy in freedom and in power. In freedom, because he was under no obligation to do that. And in
power, because his work is effective.

In his mercy God shows himself to be *righteous*. God's
righteousness is often misunderstood because we tend to
operate with an abstract idea of righteousness or justice

foreign to the biblical message. Justice in that abstract and formal sense is *suum cuique*, everyone his due: punishment for the guilty, acquittal for the innocent, reward for the deserving. That kind of justice is extremely useful in society, so long as personal relationships do not enter into the picture. But as soon as human relationships do become personal that abstract justice becomes useless. In fact, one can measure the kind of personal relationship between people by their eagerness or unwillingness to demand formal justice. Total strangers are almost bound to demand it. Members of one family will rarely take each other to court. Most relationships are somewhere in between. Paul regards it as an offence against the Christian fellowship if Christians take each other to court (1 Corinthians 6: 1-11).

For if there is a personal relationship between people, and something goes wrong, and one offends the other, then there is not just the infringement of a rule, for which just punishment can be given, nor is it merely a question of damages to be awarded. A person has been offended or harmed, a relationship has been broken. And how the relationship can be restored is largely up to the people involved. There is nothing wrong, there is nothing unjust about one being sorry and the other forgiving, and the two starting afresh. Formal justice comes in only if for some reason the relationship cannot be restored or if there never was that kind of personal relationship.

In any case the Bible does not use the word righteousness in that abstract sense. A just judge is not so much one who punishes the wicked as one who protects the innocent and the weak. A just society is not one in which everyone gets what he deserves but one in which all get their fair share, that is to say the share that God wants them to have. Almsgiving is not regarded as 'charity' but as righteousness: one gives to the poor what they ought to have because God wants them to have their fair share.

God's righteousness is therefore not his conforming to some abstract ideal outside or even above him. God is

R.R.—H

righteous in that he carries out his promise.[9] God's righteousness is his creative saving act.[10] He sees to it that in the end man gets what he wants him to have. It does not exclude his wrath and his judgment.[11] Nevertheless it means first and foremost that God abides by his covenant[12] and grants us that fellowship with himself which he intends us to have. It is his will that there should be this fellowship, this relationship of love and trust between him and us, and he sees his plan through, no matter how much opposition and injustice has to be overcome, and no matter what the cost.

That implies the forgiveness of sin. Forgiveness of sin does not mean that sin does not matter. How much sin matters to God is shown by the fact of the cross. Moreover, if sin did not matter there would be nothing to forgive. But sin destroys the relationship with God. It is responsible for a world in which there is no room for God. It creates the situation in which Christ cries out, 'My God, my God, why hast thou forsaken me?'

Nor does it mean that we can get away with sin. The risen Christ himself is the living sign that we do not get away with it. Sin does not achieve its aim. Putting someone to death is indeed the most effective method of dealing with him and disposing of him. But with Christ it just does not work. God is not so easily disposed of: he sees his plan through and raises Christ from the dead.

But there is another sense in which we do not get away with sin. Man is responsible for his actions. God wants him to be responsible: that is one of the crowning glories of his humanity. There are certain inevitable consequences of what we are and what we do. We are not suggesting that if he so wishes, God could not absolve us from the consequences of our actions. But the fact is that he holds us responsible.

Forgiveness means that in spite of everything God still accepts us as one of the family and will stand by us. It is in his fellowship and solidarity with his people that he takes full responsibility for us, for what we are and what we do. If that sounds contradictory, then it is only because we are caught

in a net of individualism and formal justice. There is really
nothing contradictory in those who belong together, though
being fully responsible for their own actions, sharing the
responsibility and being responsible for one another. There
is nothing contradictory, in such a relationship, in the One
standing for all, and God taking full responsibility for those
who are themselves responsible.

We are not speaking here of a mere theory. This is rather
something that takes place in action. How such solidarity of
guilt can work among people may be shown by just one
example. Some time ago a minister had arranged to assist a
minister abroad for a short period during the holidays. But
through the death of the incumbent he suddenly found himself in charge of a church which, though not very different
from his own in doctrine, had quite different customs. One
of the first duties he had to perform was that of giving
communion to a dying patient. He had a printed order of
service, and this demanded that the patient should make a
confession and receive absolution before receiving the sacra-
ment. But the patient was already unconscious. In his own
church private confession and communion of the dying were
rare, and it would never have occurred to anyone to communicate someone who was unconscious. Of course, the
situation was not unique, it must have happened thousands
of times before, and he knew there must be a 'correct' way of
dealing with it. But he did not know what the 'correct' way
was, and he had no time to contact his nearest colleague to
find out. He had to make his own decision. And he decided
that the only thing he could do was to make the confession
himself (in general terms, of course, as he did not know the
patient). What made him decide was this. Though the
patient was not known to him, she was one of his people. For
better or worse she and he, and the whole church, belonged
together. Her sins were his sins. He found out afterwards
that his decision was the 'correct' one. But that is not really
relevant. What is relevant is that he was suddenly made to
realize what Christian fellowship really means: that we

belong together. That, though everyone is responsible for his own actions, there is a deeper level at which we are responsible for each other.

In that sense Christ and his people belong together. In becoming one of us he does not merely share our 'human nature' but our human existence and our guilt, with its consequences. Note how he refuses to allow himself to be called 'good' (Mark 10: 18, a saying that could scarcely have become part of the tradition without any foundation in fact). Note also his cry on the cross, 'My God, my God, why hast thou forsaken me?' (Mark 15: 34). We are, of course, aware that the words are a quotation from a psalm which speaks of faith and ends in hope; nevertheless the psalm is a prayer from the depth of the human situation.

The death of Christ is therefore an inevitable part of God's act of forgiveness: it is the manner in which he identifies himself with us completely. In his righteousness God sticks to us, whatever we are and whatever we do (Romans 8: 33), even though that means getting involved in our sin and its consequences. And as he has now taken the responsibility, he will see us through.

If what we have said is true, then God's forgiveness is made effective in the cross, but the cross is not the meriting cause of his forgiveness. We ought therefore to have a look at one of the key words of the New Testament and especially of Paul, namely 'justification'.

The word 'justification' is often interpreted as suggesting that the cross is the meriting cause of God's forgiveness. It has indeed also been regarded as God's work in us by which he makes the sinner righteous, but it is usually understood to mean his verdict by which he declares us righteous, though we are not. There can be little doubt that the word is a forensic term, that it was borrowed from the court-room and that therefore it does not primarily refer to God's work in us. God does, in fact, change people and make them righteous, and that is closely connected with the justification of the sinner. But when the New Testament writers speak of God justifying the sinner, that is not what they are referring to. They have something else in mind.

The usual meaning of 'justify' is 'to pronounce a verdict of "not guilty".' In traditional Christian doctrine justification is consequently interpreted as God's verdict of not guilty. However, it is obvious that such a verdict could not possibly be based on our innocence. On the other hand it would be extremely difficult to imagine that God could base his verdict on a fiction or a lie. The interpretation of justification as a verdict of not guilty therefore requires some explanation. Such an explanation was found in a theory that describes how, and in some forms even explains why, man's guilt is transferred to the innocent Son of God, who 'paid the price of sin', and how his innocence and righteousness are transferred to us. The theory has found many able exponents from Augustine onwards but was given its classic form by Anselm of Canterbury.[13]

Anselm regards sin as an offence against God's honour. The honour which God demands is that every rational creature owes him entire subjection to his will. He who pays is righteous, he who does not pay sins. And as God must defend his honour, so he must demand restitution from those who have not paid. But man cannot give such restitution: he has nothing to give that does not already belong to God. A perfect, sinless man could give his life but there is no such man, and the lives of sinners are already forfeit. God himself could give the satisfaction that he requires. But the satisfaction must be given by man. It is therefore necessary that the Saviour should be both true God and real man, and Jesus Christ is that Saviour.

Anselm's theory of satisfaction has not been adopted without some adjustments, and the idea of the necessity of satisfaction in particular has usually been reduced to its suitability, its *convenientia*, but even so Anselm's theory has dominated Christian thought ever since.

The theory has some obvious advantages, not the least being that it emphasizes the seriousness of sin. Nevertheless there are serious objections. The doctrine of satisfaction is something that comes as an addition to the actual facts of the cross and the resurrection. It presumes that God's revelation did not take place in the actual events of the life, death and resurrection of Christ but is contained in a theory only loosely connected with the events. For not only is the theory extraneous to the events, but it does not arise naturally from them. It derives, in fact, from abstract notions of honour and righteousness foreign to the Bible. And it attempts to fit the events into a scheme that could be devised without any knowledge of the events. It is significant that Anselm develops his scheme *remoto Christo*, without Christ. The theory is worked out without any reference to the events, and the author comes to them only at the end.

It is often argued that the theory is revealed separately by God in various writings of the New Testament. That seems to imply an unbiblical understanding of revelation. God does not reveal theories but himself. But the New Testament does not, in fact, contain any such theory. Paul is often charged with the responsibility for it, but it cannot be found in his writings.[14]

Secondly, the Lord offers peace with God without any such theory. There is no suggestion in the Gospels that Jesus regarded satisfaction as a necessary condition of forgiveness. It has therefore been said that, if the theory, as is sometimes suggested, is the heart of the Christian faith, this would mean that what the Founder of Christianity taught was not Christianity at all.[15] Strictly speaking Jesus was not the 'Founder of Christianity': Jesus was not the first *Christian*, he was the *Christ*.[16] Nevertheless it would be rather strange if the heart of the Christian faith was the opposite of what Christ taught.

Thirdly, the theory is precisely what it claims not to be: a theology of the forensic fiction.

But the most serious objection is that it does not only rest on a formal idea of justice foreign to the Bible but credits God with the terrible prerogative of being unable to forgive.[17]

The language of the court is, of course, a parable. It is not meaningless but should be handled with care. The very idea of the justification of the unjust is a paradox.[18] That should make us realize the limitations of the terms employed.

Justification is not the same as forgiveness. Indeed, in a criminal case they are mutually exclusive. The accused can either be found not guilty and leave the court without any blame attached to his name, or be found guilty and then, perhaps, depending on certain circumstances, apply for pardon, and maybe receive it. But he cannot have it both ways. If justification and forgiveness were identical, then the justification of the sinner would be a legal fiction.

However, not every court case is a criminal case. In some ways the New Testament reference to the justification of the sinner is reminiscent of a civil lawsuit concerning the ownership of a slave. The proper question would then be, not, is the slave guilty? but, to whom does he belong? Parallel with this are the numerous references to redemption, that is to say, the purchase of a slave, not to keep him in slavery but to set him free: the redeemed sinner is no longer a slave of sin but a child of God.

It is doubtful if ancient Hebrew law knew the distinction between criminal and civil law which the Romans and we take for granted. The Old Testament contains some examples which may help us better to understand the message of justification.

In 1 Kings 3: 16-27, Solomon has to decide to which of two mothers a particular child belongs. The right decision has no connexion with any guilt on the part of the child. What leads to the righteous decision is the willingness of the mother to suffer: precisely the willingness to lose the child in order to save it shows that it belongs to her.

The second example deals with the question from the other side. The introduction to the Book of Job is, of necessity, couched in mythological language. It speaks of the heavenly court where Satan, the accuser, accuses Job before God. The accusation is quite specific: Job is not righteous in that he is not one of God's own: he serves God as a mercenary, one who knows which side his bread is buttered on (Job 1: 10-11). In the story Job will therefore have to be justified, that is to say, it has to be shown beyond doubt that he belongs to God. Though Job is accused the case is really directed against God: Satan disputes God's claim that Job is his. And it is Job who has to justify God's claim.

That is a tremendous task, especially as Job does not know what is going on in the heavenly court. He only knows what is happening to him. He realizes that God must be involved but he does not know how. But as he does not like what is happening to him, he says so. Being a man of God he does not hesitate to take his complaints to God. He is not a mercenary who knows which side his bread is buttered on and keeps his mouth shut. Nor is he a slave who is afraid to speak his mind. He belongs to the family and tells God what he thinks. On the ordinary religious premises that was about the most foolish thing that he could do. In a context of formal justice, in a legalistic relation in which every action must be accounted for and every sin be punished, every word Job speaks would have increased his guilt. If ever prizes were awarded for blasphemy Job would have won first prize. No wonder his friends feel that he is beyond praying for.

Yet Job is justified. Not because he said the right things. Indeed he did not. If ever a man needed forgiveness Job did. But all that he said was spoken in a living relationship with God. He was one of God's own and acted as one. A rebellious, irreverent and blasphemous member of the family, but still one of the family, one of God's own. And God is not ashamed of him but gladly claims him for his own.

The third story is the conversation between God and Abraham in Genesis 18: 23-32. The crucial verse is verse 24: 'Suppose there are fifty righteous within the city; wilt thou then destroy the place and not spare it for the fifty righteous who are in it?' The suggestion is not that God should segregate the righteous from the wicked, save the righteous and destroy the others. It is rather that, for better or worse, the people of the city belong together, and that the city, in its entirety, should be saved for the sake of the righteous, however few, fifty, or forty-five, or forty, or thirty, or twenty, or even ten. Abraham knows, of course, that it is not for him to tell God what to do. But should not the Judge of all the earth do right? This is indeed vicarious righteousness: the many are saved through the righteousness of the few (that in the story as it stands they were not saved is because there were not even those few; Lot and some of his family were saved because they did not belong to the city).

Besides that teaching of corporate responsibility and vicarious righteousness, and even vicarious suffering, there is in the Old Testament also a side that emphasizes the responsibility of the individual. We cannot solve that paradox by regarding the individualism as a later and 'higher' development. Over against the individualism of an Ezekiel we find the Songs of the Servant in Deutero-Isaiah with their message that God saves the many on account of the righteousness and the sufferings of the one.

Against this background much of the gospel becomes much clearer. In Christ God claims us for his own even if we do not act as one of the family. Even if we are prepared to disown him he is not prepared to disown us. In that respect the gospel goes much further than the Book of Job and is closer to the Songs of the Servant.

One might argue that God could in any case claim us for his own: he made us and his we are (Psalm 100: 3). But that would only make us his property, his slaves. That we are his own in a deeper sense, that we are children and heirs, that is the claim he makes on us. And that claim he justifies by standing by us, sticking to us, suffering for us and even suffering at our hands, forgiving us and always accepting full responsibility for us.

Christ did indeed take our sins upon himself, and we do indeed receive his righteousness. Not, however, by transfer but by solidarity. He became one of us, for better or worse, and thus made our condition his own. And by claiming us for his own he restores the relationship between God and us, and thus makes us righteous before God.

Thus God remains *faithful* to us and to his own intentions. God's faithfulness is an important word in the Old Testament. It is also frequently referred to in the preaching of Jesus, notably in the three parables of Luke 15, the Lost Sheep, the Lost Coin and the Prodigal Son, and, on careful examination, throughout the Gospels though the word is not actually used. But more than in his words that faithfulness is revealed by his constant fidelity to his own disciples and to the world, both before and after his resurrection. He does not let go. He holds on.

In that fidelity of Christ's we have God's own faithfulness. It was he who raised Jesus Christ from the dead. A god who would not raise Jesus Christ from the dead, a god who was not faithful, a god who could abandon the work of his hands, would not be the living God.[19] But God did raise Jesus Christ from the dead and revealed his faithfulness and righteousness.

Both in his preaching and work and in his passion and his resurrection Christ shows us the *patience* of God's love. That patience is illustrated admirably in the parable of the Prodigal Son. What patience is needed for a father to give his son his share and let him go, waiting patiently for him to return. The father did not, in fact, cut all ties, he did not disown his son. There was still something that bound the son to the father's house, but it was little more than a memory. He was let out not only on a very long leash but on one that was also very thin. Of course we must not treat the parable as an allegory. There are some things about the father which are not true of God. Moreover, we should not forget that the 'younger son' would remind the first hearers of the Gentile world rather than an ungodly individual. Still, the Gentile world is mankind without the living God, and the parable is a picture of human life without God. It is really astounding how much liberty God does give man: not only the liberty to master the world but also the liberty to disown, deny and forget God, the liberty to live without God. We are indeed let out on a very long and very thin leash. We can stray from God, we can disown and deny him, we can forget all about him, we can regard him as dead. And nothing happens. He just waits. Even after the clash of Golgotha nothing seems to happen. Christ was indeed raised from the dead but his enemies are not made aware of it.

Yet that patience is not inactive. God is patient and can wait. But Jesus Christ was raised from the dead, appeared to his disciples and sent them out to claim the world for him. Even so that is done only by means of the word, through the proclamation of the message, not by force.

Not by force. But still with sovereign *power*. It is usual to speak of God as all-powerful. We call him 'Almighty God'. But omnipotence is an abstraction, and we should note that, strictly speaking, it is not found in the original texts either of the Bible or of the Creed. 'I believe in God, the Father Almighty', is a not quite accurate rendering, second-hand, through the Latin,[20] of an original Greek that means, 'I believe in God, the Father, the Ruler of all'. The word *Pantokrator*, 'Ruler of all', is used in the Greek Old Testament as a translation of *Shaddai*,[21] one of God's names, of uncertain meaning, and as a rendering of *sebaot*,[22] '(Lord) of hosts'. In the New Testament it is found in 2 Corinthians 6: 18, which is a quotation from the Old Testament,[23] and several times in the Revelation to John. Revelation 4: 8 quotes the Old Testament (Isaiah 6: 3); *Pantokrator* should here be rendered, 'the Lord of hosts'. The same translation seems to be demanded for Revelation 11: 17; 15: 3; 21: 22. That leaves Revelation 16: 14 and 19: 15, where the word is used of God the Father, and Revelation 1: 8, where it refers to the risen Christ. For an understanding of those passages, where there is no parallel with the Old Testament, we have to consider what the Revelation to John is about. It is a revelation, in the form of a number of visions,[24] of the risen Christ as the one who is in command and eventually overcomes all opposition. That seems to suggest that the term *Pantokrator* does not mean to convey the notion of an abstract omnipotence but rather the notion of God's actual and factual ability to see his plans through. Such an interpretation seems particularly obvious in Revelation 19: 6, but also in Revelation 1: 8; 11: 17; 16: 14. It is interesting to note that, while Christian theologians were busy turning God's omnipotence into an abstraction, artists long continued to present Christ the *Pantokrator* as we find him in the Revelation to John.[25]

That book presents a grand vision of the sovereign power of the risen Christ. Its impact on us is not so immediate as it must have been on the first readers. But it is based on a real encounter with the risen Lord and the author wants to present Christ in his risen power.

In the resurrection of Christ God reveals himself as the One who is able to see his plan through. The enmity of the world, the power of evil active in that enmity, and death itself are overcome.

This part of the message tends to be misunderstood on account of our human disinclination to take death seriously. Men have always found it difficult to accept death. One of the most attractive aspects of religion, one that plays a large part in giving it its hold over people, is that it seems to guarantee an escape from death. The *rites de passage* by which primitive man moves smoothly not only from one stage of life to another but also from one life to the next, the pyramids which were to ensure the pharaoh's next life, the Upanishadic teaching of *samsara*,[26] the widespread belief that Christianity's prime function is to provide the faithful with front seats in heaven, they all witness to man's deep-seated belief that death must not be real, that it cannot be real, that, indeed, it is not real.

The faith of Israel, as represented by the Old Testament,

has been extremely wary of such beliefs. There is, in fact, no trace of them in the Old Testament, and such traces as there are in the New Testament are accidental and superficial (see pages 68ff.).[27] In the Bible death is the end. Resurrection is the impossible. But in Jesus Christ God has done the impossible.

Through the resurrection of Christ we thus know that God is able to do what he wills and that, indeed, he does the impossible.

Those who have met God in Jesus Christ know that his will is the will of his love. It is God's will to have his people for himself. It is his will to have fellowship with us, to stand by us and to see us through. The power of God is not the blind force of destiny but power to save.[28]

That power to save in the face of all resistance is shown not only in that victory over death by which God has undone the work of those who crucified the Lord and by which he overcame death itself, but also in the fact that there are people who believe. For this is the hardest resistance: the resistance in ourselves. Nothing could indeed be more impossible than that such people as we are could ever be reconciled to God and drawn into the reach of his love. Faith itself is the most remarkable evidence of God's power to do the impossible.

It would be mistaken to interpret the preceding in individualistic terms. God's love is concerned with all that he has made. It is his will to restore the whole of his creation to the right relationship with himself and thereby to true life and happiness. To those who have met the Lord there can be no doubt that he will overcome all resistance, that he will reconcile all things to himself, that he will make all things new. That is his will, and he is in a position to do what he wills.

This God is a God who is not far off but who is *present*. The usual term is omnipresent: God is present at all times in all places; his presence pervades everything. That is a wonderful idea but rather abstract (though, curiously, it has been criticized for not being sufficiently abstract). In the resurrection of Christ God reveals himself as the One who is present in a more direct but also a more incidental sense. In the resurrection stories Christ is present, not vaguely, always and everywhere, but directly, concretely, at particular times in particular places. It is indeed suggested that the Lord may be there even when the disciples are not aware of him. One of the striking points in the story of Thomas is that Jesus knows what Thomas said even when he seemed not to be present (John 20: 27, see page 31). In the Gospel according to Matthew the Lord promises to be present with those who meet in his name (Matthew 18: 20) and to be with his people all the days, every one of them, until the end of the (present) age (Matthew 28: 20[29]). But there is no general doctrine of his omnipresence.

That is entirely in line with the Old Testament teaching about God's presence. That has found classic expression in Psalm 139. There the Psalmist does not speak of God's omnipresence in an abstract and general sense. But, wherever he moves he finds that God is there. The presence of God is not diffuse but concrete.

It is not necessarily mistaken to speak of God's omnipresence any more than it is to speak of his omnipotence. But it has its peculiar dangers. A God who is omnipresent in a vague and general sense is no longer able to withdraw. Such a god is a 'universal' being instead of the God and Father of our Lord Jesus Christ. He can no longer call us to himself because he is everywhere. He can no longer gather us round the Lord Jesus Christ because we can find him anywhere. That does not necessarily follow from the use of the word, but the danger is certainly there.

Therefore it is better to say, with the New Testament, that God is in Christ, and that, in Christ, he is with us. Then, even if we cannot find him, we can be confident that he can find us.

4. JESUS CHRIST: THE TRUTH ABOUT MAN

The resurrection of Christ relates the whole of the earthly life of Jesus to its origin in God.[1] It therefore gives a special significance to that earthly life. We must emphasize that it was a *human* life, that it was precisely not a divine or a semi-divine life. Jesus Christ therefore not only shows us who God is but also what man is in God's intentions, what he is in his present condition, and what he will be.

Jesus shows us what man is in God's intentions. It cannot be emphasized too much that Jesus was a man, an ordinary man, subject to the same limitations as other men (see pages 106ff.). One might indeed say that he was the only normal man, in that he lived a life of faith and obedience, the kind of life God intended for us, the kind of life for which we were made. That does, indeed, make him different from others, but different in action, not in 'substance', not in 'nature'.

In Paul's writings we find the expression 'the second Adam'. The term seems to pose particular problems in view of the fact that we regard Adam as a legendary, Jesus as an historic figure. But the problems are really only apparent. For, though Paul did regard Adam as an actual figure from the past, his function in Paul's theology is mythical. Adam stands for Everyman: Adam before the fall is man as God intended him, Adam after the fall is man in his actual condition.

That condition is one of estrangement from God. It is a condition into which all of us are born. But it is not as if we inherit sin from our parents in the same way as we inherit the colour of our skin or the traits of our character. It is inherited in the manner in which we inherit our country, with its language, customs and traditions. They are no part of our natural make-up, and if our parents had moved before we were born they would not have been ours in the same way; yet our country, its traditions and customs and its way of life are very much our own.

Like every other human being Jesus was born into that condition of sin and estrangement from God. He differed from others in what he did in that condition: he lived a perfect human life in faith and obedience, according to God's intentions. His life is therefore the normal human life by which all the others can be judged. We can say that without having recourse to a negative concept of sinlessness. The perfection of Jesus is not that he lacked something called sin, present in the lives of other people, but that, in practice, he acted according to God's will.

Naturally we must not overlook the fact that we are not speaking of an abstract human ideal but of a concrete man living in a concrete situation. Like every human life his was unique in that the situations in which he found himself were unrepeatable. His faith and obedience are repeatable, at least in principle, but it would be absurd to copy the concrete decisions he had to make and the specific actions he had to carry out.

That perfect life of faith and obedience that he lived shows the paradox of the human condition. The 'sin of Adam', the human condition, is a condition in which everyone is estranged from God. We are manifestly unable not to sin.[2] But the life of Christ shows that that inability is not an inescapable fate. Sin is our fault. We are guilty.

It would be a mistake to regard Paul's reference to the 'sin of Adam' as an explanation of sin, an attempt to seek the cause of sin somewhere outside ourselves and thus excuse ourselves. The story of Genesis 3 takes great pains to lay the responsibility squarely at man's door, and every sin in the following chapters of Genesis is an action by itself. Paul would not quarrel with that. In Adam all have sinned inasmuch as they actually did sin.[3]

There is, as we saw, not only a condition of sin, a condition in which all men sin, but also a solidarity of sin, and consequently of guilt, from which no one escapes. We belong together and are responsible for each other: all for one and one for all. It is part of Christ's humanity that he shares in that responsibility (see page 116) and takes the consequences even to the death on the cross. Paul can therefore say that he came in the sinful flesh (Romans 8: 3) and even that he was made sin for us (2 Corinthians 5: 21).

But in that human condition of sin, in the sinful flesh, in solidarity with this world of sinners, and bearing full responsibility for the sins of the world, Jesus Christ lived that unique life of faith and obedience.

Faith is a relationship in which two persons can trust each other and rely on each other. The relationship is difficult to describe because essentially it is such a simple one. Jesus knows that he can rely on the Father, and the Father can rely on him. Totally uncomplicated.

This relationship becomes active in obedience. If you trust someone implicitly you are prepared to carry out his will. Obedience of this kind is always concrete obedience. It is not confined to living by certain standards or according to certain general commandments. It is knowing at every moment what God's will is in this particular situation, and carrying it out.

A good example from the Gospels is the Gethsemane story (Mark 14: 32-43). There we find Jesus waiting a long time, knowing full well that Judas knows the place and is on his way to betray him. There was plenty of time to make his escape. Nothing would have been easier than just leaving the garden with his disciples and disappearing in the night. And there is no general commandment that tells people to wait for their enemies and court disaster. Nor was there any particular moral merit in waiting to be taken prisoner and facing the cross. Generally speaking it is not advisable, morally or otherwise, to act in the way Jesus did. It would have been wiser and, generally speaking, better to make his escape and to organize his followers elsewhere. The agony in the garden is concerned with precisely this: finding out if the cross was the road he had to take. But once he knew that staying and waiting, and allowing himself to be captured and killed was what God wanted of him now, at this precise moment, he stayed and waited. Concrete obedience to God means knowing the *kairos*, the precise moment, and what God demands at this precise moment.

Knowing God's will is, of course, not always a matter of sudden inspiration. It is often mediated through very mundane means. It often comes from looking at any situation very carefully and from a real concern for other people and their needs. It is to some extent what is now often called 'situation ethics', but without the human autonomy which the latter term implies. And it is real service. The servant of God is the servant of men: 'the Son of man also came not to be served but to serve' (Mark 10: 45). The life of Jesus was truly a life of service, a life for others.[4]

What we have said is not affected by the fact that our knowledge of the life of Jesus is limited and that the known facts are not sufficient to give us the material for a biography or for a study of his personality. What we are concerned with is his work and the impact he made through his word and actions both on those who met him during his earthly life and on those who have got to know him since. Through mere information one can learn much about a person. But one can only know a person—as opposed to knowing something about him—through the encounter with him. That encounter may be a mediated one—through reading the Gospels. This, in fact, is precisely what the writers of the Gospels want to achieve: that, through reading the Gospels, one should encounter the living Christ. They do not want to give information about him, though the Gospels do contain certain information about his earthly life: they want to present him to us.

It is true, even of the secular study of history, that it is incomplete if it remains confined to the collection of facts from the past and a knowledge of people and events from that past. The study of history is something different from building in the mind a museum of antiquities or a collection of models. Without a real confrontation with people and an element of dialogue history is dead, as everybody knows who has ever been made to suffer the wrong kind of history teaching. People, even people from the past who have long been dead, cannot be mere objects.[5]

Thus the picture that we are given of Jesus is a sketch, not of his biography, nor of his personality, but of Jesus as he was, and still is, actually met. The Gospels do not reproduce him, they present him, the one normal man, the man in God's image, the man of God's intentions, who is at the same time the man for others.

In Jesus we are confronted with the normal man, whose humanity is the same as our own. Yet it is obvious, painfully obvious, how different he was from ourselves. And that not because of some metaphysical extra, 'because he was the Son of God', but because in his ordinary humanity, within the same framework in which our own lives are lived, he lived that life of complete faith and perfect obedience. We realize that, not by contemplating his life and comparing it with our own, but by the actual confrontation with him. Dorothy Sayers has caught this admirably in a phrase she puts on Matthew's lips: 'Ah! makes you feel bad, he does, sometimes. Laughs and talks and eats with you—and all the time you know you're not fit to touch him . . .'[6]

We are not expected to be superhuman and to live superhuman lives. We are human and are expected to live human lives. The confrontation shows our lives up for what they are: less than human.

That confrontation reaches its climax in the events leading up to the cross. The cross was due, not to some dark destiny or some eternal decree, but to the actions of ordinary responsible people. He had to die, not because a divine law decreed it but because Caiaphas and Pilate and the others involved were what they were, that is to say, because people are what they are, because we are what we are. That does not mean that the cross was not part of God's design. But it does mean that we cannot use God's design as an excuse to deny our own responsibility.

In view of that it is not really very important to find out who was more to blame, Caiaphas *cum suis* or Pilate. It is perhaps necessary, in view of the traditional custom of attributing the death of Christ to 'the Jews', that we should not underestimate Pilate's part in the event.[7] But it is much more important that we should realize that those involved in the historical event were people like ourselves, that we are united with them in a solidarity of guilt, that, as the poet Revius put it, 'It's not the Jews, Lord Jesu, who crucified thee ... It's not the soldiers ... It's I who did this to thee ...'[8] Man is the cause of the cross, and that means concretely that we are responsible.

And that not through any imperfection in our make-up but through wrong relationships. That man is a sinner is not a statement about his nature but about his actual life. There is nothing wrong with human nature, that same nature in which Jesus Christ lived his life of complete faith and perfect obedience. Where we are wrong is in our relationships with God and with one another and in our relation to the world and our task. It is there that we fail God.

It is remarkable how active Christianity has been in laying the blame outside ourselves. No theologian of repute has actually made God the author of sin. But we do like to think that somehow human nature is at fault and that man cannot really help being a sinner. Perhaps it is our 'physical nature' that drags us down (and how wonderful will it be when we are no longer burdened with that!). Or we say that the fall destroyed or damaged the image of God and changed our nature so that we are no longer capable of not sinning. And we like to think of Christ as being not really human, as somehow incapable of sinning, so that his perfect obedience can no longer be a judgment and a challenge.

But though it is true that we are no longer free not to sin, that slavery is no part of our make-up, of our nature, it is a condition in which we find ourselves and from which we cannot escape, and often do not even wish to escape.

Nevertheless we are still the object of God's love. We have broken our relationship with him but he remains the same towards us. And the risen Lord restores the relationship between God and ourselves. We have already seen how the appearances of the risen Lord restored the relationship with his disciples (pages 78-85). We now have to go one step further. Confrontation with the living Lord means, to everyone who believes, being drawn into a living relationship with the living God.

That implies a number of things. It implies the forgiveness of sins inasmuch as God is willing to hold on to us and maintain his relationship with us even though we have broken off the relationship.

It implies the justification of the sinner inasmuch as God declares that in spite of our transgressions we are still his own. We are righteous in that he still regards us as his own: that is, after all, all the justification we need. And that is obviously not our own righteousness, for our sin is precisely that we have broken our relationship with him and deny that we are his own. It is a righteousness which is given to us. It is the justification of the sinner which means that we are both righteous and sinners.

It implies faith inasmuch as there is no way that leads from us to God. Only he himself can make himself known to us. Through God alone can God be known.[9] Faith is a manner of knowing someone that is entirely dependent on its object.[10] Faith can only be given (see pages 72-7).

Inasmuch as faith can only be given it implies election. The choice is in God's hands. That those who belong to Christ belong to God is his choice, not ours. And again, it is God's decision who belong to Christ (compare John 15: 16). That does not mean that we have to settle for a deterministic view of the world. But it does mean that our condition is one in which we are entirely dependent on God's mercy. Knowing God's mercy as revealed in Christ, that is not a bad condition to be in.

That raises some serious questions. Is it God's will that some should know him and others should not? Is it his choice that some should be saved and others should not? Those and similar questions have caused endless controversy in the Church.

However, there is really no answer to such questions. It is indeed said in the New Testament that it is God's will that all men should be saved and arrive at the knowledge of truth (1 Timothy 2: 4), and Paul's theology on the whole tends towards a belief in the apocatastasis, the restoration of all things (compare especially Romans 9—11).[11] But he never develops that as a general theory. The New Testament generally, and the Gospels in particular, also speak at times in quite different terms, emphasizing the seriousness of God's judgment. The New Testament sayings cannot be fitted into a tidy scheme, whether universalistic or predestinarian. The authors did not see it as their task to provide a blueprint of God's counsel but to offer God's grace. Any attempt to fit the whole of the New Testament testimony into a neat comprehensive scheme is bound to go astray. We have to leave the decision to God's mercy. And that is just as well.

It also implies a new freedom. Man without Christ is not free to choose. That, again, is not a statement concerning his nature: it merely indicates the condition in which he finds himself, a condition in which he is a slave of sin and no longer free to choose for God. The term, a slave of sin, is a good one, because it describes precisely that. A slave was never fundamentally different from a free man. He differed from a free man, not in his nature, but in his condition. He was the same as a free man, only he was not free. To be sure, it was inevitable that his condition should eventually affect his character. Similarly, being a slave of sin does affect man's character. But what traditional theology calls our 'sinful nature', is neither the essence, nor the cause of sin, but its effect. Sin is simply the condition in which we are not free to choose for God.

In confronting us in Jesus Christ God has restored the relationship between him and ourselves and thereby changed the situation and our condition. We are now free to choose and live for God.

The confrontation with the living Christ is the moment of decision. Not in the sense that a free man, already gifted with a free will, meets a new person about whom he has to make up his mind. No, his freedom is something new, a gift which he receives only in the confrontation with Christ. The freedom to choose and live for God is given in that confrontation itself.[12]

That freedom, however, is not a thing. It is realized only in the act of believing. But it is a very real freedom in which we can make free and responsible decisions, not only the fundamental one to choose for God, but also the day-to-day decisions of our secular lives.

The new relationship with Christ looks forward to his future in which we shall share completely and fully that life which he lives with God. We know, more or less, what our present condition is. We can, through meeting Christ, have some idea of what God wants us to be, and therefore, as God's intentions cannot ultimately be frustrated, what we shall be. But it is impossible for us to imagine a world in which the perfect fellowship with God is restored, in which relationships between people are exactly as God intends them to be, a life in which all are at peace with God, with each other and with the world in which they live. Any attempt at describing such a world and such a human family would be bound to fail: it is something so completely foreign to our experience that our imagination simply cannot cope.

5. THE BODY OF CHRIST

We have so far referred to our relationship with Christ as

'having fellowship with him', and 'following him'. But the New Testament frequently suggests a much closer communion and indeed union between Christ and his people. Among various expressions used to indicate that closer communion Paul's 'body of Christ' is probably the most extreme. It has also been a most successful expression. Not only is it taken up in the Deutero-Pauline literature but it has played a large part in the Church's later thinking. In fact it has been so successful as to have become almost meaningless.[1]

The idea of a corporate body is quite familiar to us. It was not so in Paul's day, though it was, in fact, not entirely new. The universe could be likened to an organism, and so could a group of people. And occasionally we find the word used metaphorically to denote a group or a collection.

But Paul uses the word differently, not in a corporate but in a corporal sense: he is referring, not to a society but to a person, namely Christ.[2] The idea of people being members of a corporate body is not at all strange. But the idea of people, i.e. the believers, being parts of another person's body must have seemed absurd. Yet this is precisely how Paul uses the expression.

The expression 'the body of Christ' has obvious connexions with the Eucharist. It is clear from the records of the Last Supper that the Eucharist was not only regarded as a meal of fellowship but as a manner in which Christ gave himself to his people. There was, of course, no specific doctrine as to how that was effected. The doctrine of transubstantiation was still a matter of the future, as were the symbolic and other interpretations: they could only be the outcome of many centuries of reflection. But there is no doubt that the sharing of the elements represented Christ giving his body and blood, that is, himself, to his people.[3] Partaking of the Lord's Supper was regarded as 'feeding on Christ'.[4] At the same time the believers became identified with Christ, and it is noteworthy that 'discerning the body' of Christ (1 Corinthians 11: 29) refers to the Christian community, not to the elements of the Eucharist.

'Feeding on Christ' is, of course, not the same as becoming part of his body. But communion meals of this kind are not uncommon in other religions, and it is widely believed that 'feeding on the god' establishes an identity with the god. Such beliefs played a prominent part in the Mystery religions, which were such a notable part of the religious scene in Paul's days. It is therefore not *a priori* impossible that they played a part in the formation of Paul's belief. Nevertheless, Paul does not say, 'I am Christ', or, 'I am a Christ', but, 'you are the body of Christ and individually members of it' (1 Corinthians 12: 27). He does not identify the individual believer with Christ but identifies every believer as a part of his body. One need not deny the presence of a genuine mystical element in the expression to see that this is not mysticism in the ordinary sense of the word.

Mersch and Robinson[5] connect Paul's use of the term with his experience on the road to Damascus (Acts 9: 4f.; 22: 7f.; 26: 14f.): while persecuting the Church Paul had, in fact, been persecuting Christ. It is not entirely impossible that there is a connexion. But we should not overlook the fact that this view is based on Luke's, not Paul's account of the event. Nor should we forget that a man's representative stands for the man himself, that a good representative in a sense identifies himself with him, but is not identical with him. An ambassador stands for his government, in former days for his king. But he is not the government, he represents it. Similarly, the Christian community can stand for Christ without necessarily being identical with him.

It is tempting to connect the references to Christ as the head of the body with the widespread use of the word, in Hebrew[6] as in other languages, for the head of a community. But that would mean disregarding the corporal, not just corporate, sense in which Paul seems to speak of the body of Christ.

What makes a body is not just the assemblage of its parts

or even the mutual connexion, relation and limitation of the parts. What makes the body is the individuality that holds it together and governs it.[7] That Jesus Christ is the head of the Church, and that the Church is the body of Christ and the believers parts of his body means first and foremost that he is the one who binds them together and governs them, both individually and as a body.

Both in Paul's letters (1 Corinthians and elsewhere) and in the Deutero-Pauline literature (Ephesians and elsewhere) the body of Christ is held together and governed by Christ and therefore one. But the unity of the body is not primarily a matter of having the same mind and sharing the same views. It is this, that Christ is in command of the individual Christian and of the Christian community.[8] It is almost inevitable that Christians should disagree about many things, but they are still bound together by the same Christ. Any division among Christians is an offence against the body of Christ.

It is therefore not surprising that the term is used particularly, though not exclusively, in connexion with the practice of the Christian life. It determines how Christians, in spite of differences and disagreements, live together as one body. Those differences are mainly of two kinds. In the first place, various parts of the body have various functions and have therefore received various gifts. If it were not so the body could not function properly. But secondly—and here the term 'the body' is not really very helpful—various Christians receive God's gifts in various ways, on account of differences in make-up, character, upbringing, etc. Those differences are not a contribution to the riches of the Church[9] but simply reflect the human condition. Even so, they should not be allowed to interfere with the unity of the body. People can still eat and work together even if they have very different characters and very different opinions. And people can still, with all their differences, enjoy each other's company.

Eating and working together is indeed what the Christian

fellowship is about. The Eucharist is the meal that binds Christians together with their head and with each other. It should be an occasion to be enjoyed, a real celebration.[10]

But working together is the other side. The head acts through the body and its individual parts. It would be saying more than we know, if we maintained that the risen Christ has no other hands than ours. But this much is certain, that the believers are parts of his body through which he acts.

6. JESUS CHRIST THE LORD

In the risen Lord God claims us for himself. The message of the resurrection does not come to us as a mere piece of information but as a claim and a challenge. It is indeed identical with the gospel of the kingdom of God: it demands a decision, it demands faith, loyalty, obedience. When Paul speaks of his confrontation with the risen Lord (Galatians 1: 15ff.) he shows how it led him to a life of obedience. Luke, in his descriptions of the same event, makes the same point: 'You will be told what you are to do' (Acts 9: 6); 'And I said, "What shall I do, Lord?" And the Lord said to me, "Rise, and go into Damascus, and there you will be told all that is appointed for you to do" ' (Acts 22: 10); 'Wherefore, O King Agrippa, I was not disobedient to the heavenly vision' (Acts 26: 19).

The final words of the Gospel according to Matthew point the same way. It is irrelevant to ask if Jesus really did speak those precise words on that occasion. They still present the risen Lord's command to his people. 'All authority in heaven and on earth has been given to me. Go therefore and make disciples of all nations, baptizing them in the name of the Father and of the Son and of the Holy Spirit, teaching them to observe all that I have commanded you . . .' (Matthew 28: 18-20). What Jesus has been given is not just power but authority. And the teaching, the 'doctrine'[1] that has to be passed on is, 'to observe all that I have commanded you'.

And the Gospel according to John does not only refer to Christ as 'the truth' (John 14: 6) but also speaks of 'doing what is true' (John 3: 21; compare 1 John 1: 6).

The simple obedience to the living Lord is threatened in many ways. First of all there is the inclination to regard the gospel merely as the communication of certain truths. In order to speak of the message at all, the Church must needs formulate the message. She must also guard it against misrepresentation. The ideal of 'orthodoxy', the acceptance of and adherence to the right doctrine, is not an absurd one. But orthodoxy can, at best, only be a standard of the communication of the message, it can never determine whether or not a person belongs to Christ. And an emphasis on orthodoxy is fraught with serious danger. It has, in the past, often led to hunts for heretics; they have now become less frequent, though the twentieth century has not been entirely free of them. It can also result in a blind spot for the particular needs of the moment. The clergy and ministers in Germany, and also (though in extremely small numbers) in occupied Europe, who supported National Socialism, were almost without exception of the strictest orthodoxy: they adhered faithfully and meticulously to the formulations of the Christian faith framed some hundreds of years ago, but failed to see the dangers of a new movement that was, of course, not mentioned in the ancient creeds any more than it was in the Bible. They also point to another, the most fatal danger of orthodoxy, namely that not only may the assent to certain doctrinal formulations come to be regarded as the standard of one's faith but the Christian faith may come to be identified with such assent. If the faith is indeed identical with the assent to certain truths, then it becomes irrelevant how one lives and what one does. Very few have actually drawn that conclusion. Nevertheless the idea that the Christian faith essentially consists of believing certain truths or holding certain views is a constant threat to our obedience.

A second threat to our obedience is the inclination to confine the Christian faith to the 'inner life'. Historically the great emphasis on the inner life is connected with a reaction to orthodoxy. The men of the 'Further Reformation' in the Netherlands (Gisbert Voetius and others), the early Pietists in Germany (Jakob Spener, A. H. Francke, Nikolaus von Zinzendorf, and others) and the early Methodists in Great Britain (John and Charles Wesley, George Whitefield, and others) were concerned that the faith should not only be 'correct' but that it should be real. And the reality of the faith was not only a matter of the 'inner life', let alone of the emotions, though they did in fact receive a good deal of attention, but it was something that became active in practical obedience. No one can deny the enormous amount of practical Christian work that has resulted from those movements.

Even so, many of their followers were inclined to emphasize the inner life at the expense of the practice of the Christian life. And those who did understand that obedience is the form of the Christian life understood that obedience in individualistic terms. It is true that the 'do-gooder' is a caricature, but it is also true that too few Christians saw the gospel as a challenge to the society in which they lived.

That is partly, perhaps even largely, due to a neglect of the Old Testament. That neglect could take two forms. The more traditional form is that one pays lip-service to the Old Testament by regarding it as an intrinsic part of God's word but at the same time one empties it of any real significance by interpreting it merely as an introduction to the New. The New Testament was the thing that mattered, and the Old was only useful as a repository of predictions of what was to happen in the New. It was, of course, also interesting to learn how God dealt with people before he sent Christ, but the actual content of its message was not really relevant.

The other form was more radical, and consisted in a complete divorce of the New Testament from the Old.

But the Old Testament is the ground on which the New is

built. The New Testament authors take it for granted that the God who revealed himself in Jesus Christ was the God who spoke through the Old Testament. And the Lord Jesus Christ made it quite clear that he himself regarded the Old Testament in that light. That does not mean that we must necessarily share the New Testament writers' views on the Old. But it does mean that their message always implies the background of the Old and that we are bound to misinterpret them if we do not take that into account.

If, therefore, the New Testament keeps silent on some issues which play a large part in the Old, it does not follow that the New Testament authors regarded those as unimportant or that they did not share the Old Testament views concerning them. On the contrary we may rest assured that they regarded the Old Testament message on those issues as valid and authoritative. The *argumentum e silentio* is always dubious. But as the New Testament authors knew their Old Testament and took its authority for granted, their silence on many points should be regarded as an endorsement rather than a criticism of what the Old Testament says.

It is certainly interesting to note that the Old Testament was not the only world they knew, and an increased knowledge of the Hellenistic world in which the gospel was first proclaimed has given us a better understanding of certain aspects of its message. But our fascination with this interesting field of knowledge should not blind us to the fact that the New Testament has its roots in the Old. Without the Old Testament the New hangs in the air. By itself it is incomplete and lacks precisely those fundamental insights which keep it firmly on the ground.

One of the consequences of the divorce between the Testaments has been the interpretation of the gospel as a 'religion of salvation'. If it is thus interpreted, then what matters is man and his salvation and nothing else. In that respect it would be comparable to other religions of the kind, the ancient Mystery religions, Buddhism,[2] and especially the *bhakti* variety of Hinduism. But the gospel is not a 'religion of salvation'. It would indeed be true to say that the message of the cross and resurrection makes any such religion super-fluous. The gospel does not teach people how they can save themselves, nor how they can get saved. It proclaims that they are saved and that the God of their salvation claims them for his own. Its aim is not to salvage some souls from the ruin of the world but to claim the world for the living God.

The biblical message is secular. The religious man is always inclined to concern himself with the spiritual and eternal things and to let the world go to the devil, or, at best, to convert the world to a religious understanding of itself. The Old Testament is thoroughly secular in that it leaves the eternal things to God and pushes man with his nose on the earth. Secularism is not a modern invention (even though the word is): it is already one of the striking features of the Yahvist, the author (or authors) of the oldest parts of the Pentateuch. The story of the fall (Genesis 3) is concerned with a desire for a more than human existence and for super-natural knowledge: 'you will be like *Elohim*, knowing good and evil'. *Elohim*, in the Yahvist, rarely means 'God'. It usually means 'gods', that is to say, supernatural beings. Being 'like *Elohim*' therefore means being more than a human being. 'Good and evil' means 'everything':[3] the reference is to a kind of omniscience, including supernatural knowledge. The cardinal sin is not being too worldly but being too heavenly.

There is, in the Yahvist, but also in other Old Testament writers, a horror of messing about with the supernatural. A good example is the strange legend of Genesis 6: 1-4. Legends of marriages or at least intercourse between super-natural beings[4] and humans are widespread, and the Yahvist was, of course, not in a position to question such stories on rational grounds. His criticism is of a different kind. Whereas in the religions of the Gentiles such stories were a matter of great pride for the presumed offspring of those liaisons, he regards the whole business as a disgusting affair, a grave sin which he connects with the wrath of God as shown in the flood.

The eternal things are God's. Man's place and task are in the created world, to examine it, know it, work in it and master it (Genesis 2: 18-20). And so it remains throughout the Old Testament. The Priestly author(s), writing several centuries later, in the hymn of the creation, emphasizes the same point (Genesis 1: 26-31).

But the dominion of the earth, given to man, is not a mere formal mastery. The earth is the field of our obedience to God. And that also implies that man is called to work for a just society. Doing the will of God is not only a matter of private ethics, not only a task for individual do-gooders, but a responsibility of the community. There was, of course, as yet no disestablishment. Religious and secular community were identical. But whenever there was a conflict between 'Church and State', between the rulers and the exponents of God's word, the latter tended to be more secular, more concerned with a just society (very much so in the Book of Amos, but also, for instance, in the conflict between Samuel and Saul: note the part played by religious scruples both in Saul's conflict with Samuel, 1 Samuel 13: 7-15, and in his growing estrangement from his son Jonathan, 1 Samuel 14: 24-26).

Another result of the divorce is a peculiar dualism, Christian but unbiblical. It is widely taken for granted that matter, though rarely regarded as evil, is of lesser value than the things spiritual; that the body is the seat of our 'lower nature', and that our 'immortal soul' is of immeasurably greater importance. Indeed some translators have not hesitated to introduce such notions into their versions of the New Testament.[5]

There is, however, no evidence to suggest that our Lord or the New Testament authors questioned the Old Testament understanding of the world as essentially good. Nor is there any evidence that they did not regard the earth and the world of men as the proper field of our activity and of our obedience to God.

It is true that the hope of the life everlasting appears only on the fringe of the Old Testament, whereas it has a prominent place in the New. But in the New Testament the hope of the life to come is God's gift, something that we cannot achieve for ourselves but that God has already achieved for us. Naturally it is not suggested that the 'inner life' is no concern of ours, and we are indeed called to repent, to work for the treasure that does not perish and even, though only once, for our salvation. But, and this is surely significant, we are called to work our own salvation *because God works in us both the will and the work* (Philippians 2: 12-13; some translations are not very precise). Moreover we should surely ask ourselves if the 'treasures in heaven' (Matthew 6: 20) really are a reward to be received when the present life is over, 'a front seat in heaven', or the reward which we receive in having the proper relationship with God here and now. But perhaps the two cannot be so neatly separated.

No doubt the Last Judgment is presented as relating to our actions in the present life (Matthew 25: 31-46). However, that does not mean that we should conduct our lives in view of that, and it does not detract from the fact that even in such passages as Matthew 25: 31-46 man's proper field of action is the created world. When we are enjoined to 'seek first his kingdom and his righteousness' (Matthew 6: 33), we should remember that the kingdom of God is realized in the obedience of his people (see page 79).[6] Whatever the eschatological overtones of the expression, that is how the hearers would understand it.

In the New Testament the social implications are not stressed. They would be taken for granted as part of the Old Testament message. But the early Christians were not in a position to have much influence on the structure of the society in which they lived. The only practical possibility was to redress the effects of social injustice within their own circle, as far as possible. But the expectation of the just society was not lost.

The secular character of the message does not mean that God takes second place. On the contrary, it means that he is taken seriously as the Ruler of all.

It is curious to see how religious people are for ever doing the things they ought not to do and not doing the things they ought to do, not only in that, in a moral sense, they often do the wrong things and do not do the right things (that is something they have in common with everybody else), but in that they are for ever asking God to do the things they could perfectly well do for themselves and should be doing for themselves, while they spend a lot of effort on trying to do what God has already done for them. The eternal things, including our salvation, are safely in God's hands. There is nothing we can do that has not already been done, indeed there is nothing we can do at all in that field. Our proper field of activity is the created world. It is there that God commands us to do his will and it is there that we ought to work. His command does indeed include the spreading of the gospel, but even that is not a matter of 'saving souls' (that has already been done) but of telling people that God so loved the world that he gave his son, and even that is done by secular means.

There is a story about Claus Harms, how he, who used to work hard on his sermons, was once persuaded by a more religious friend to leave it all to the Holy Ghost and refrain from such preparation. On Sunday, as he entered his pulpit, he prayed the Holy Ghost to speak to him. And indeed, the Holy Ghost did speak, and said, 'Claus, you have been lazy'. The spreading and preaching of the gospel is indeed a work that Christ does through his Spirit. Yet the people whom he uses in that work have to do their job carefully, using all the means at their disposal, in an entirely secular manner. And the same thing applies to our secular jobs. It is often said that farmers today no longer need God because they have fertilizer. But that only shows that before they had fertilizer they entirely misunderstood their own part in God's creation.

The mastery of the created world is a job given to man to perform. That mastery is incomplete, but that should only spur him on to learn more about the world in which he lives, to find new and better techniques, and increase his mastery of the world. But he should not regard God as a substitute for the techniques he has not yet mastered, as an explanation of the things he has not yet been able to explain, or as an expedient to do what he himself is too lazy to do. Increasing man's knowledge and mastery of the created world is part of our Christian obedience (Genesis 1: 28, and elsewhere). It is, of course, also a natural desire, but this natural desire is part of man's God-given make-up.

But Christian obedience does not stop there. Our obedience to God is shown also, and particularly, in what we do with our knowledge and ability.

It is often assumed that Christian obedience consists of abiding by certain commandments, standards and principles. The Ten Commandments especially have functioned in the Church as a rule for the Christian life: as they express God's will, Christian obedience should be determined by them.

But that means a misunderstanding of their proper function. The Ten Commandments, or any law for that matter, can only have a limiting function. They describe the outlines of the area within which a life of obedience to God is to be lived. But they do not and cannot fill the area within those outlines. That is why they are mainly negative.

It is perfectly possible for a person or a community not to serve any gods beside the living God, and yet to fall short of true service of the living God (Exodus 20: 1-3). It is very possible to refrain from adultery and yet fail to make a success of one's marriage (verse 14). One can very easily be unconcerned about someone's good name without actually slandering him (verse 16). These, and the other commandments set certain limits but cannot by themselves fill the Christian life.

That does not detract from their significance. It is important for us to know the limits beyond which there can be neither true freedom nor true obedience. Moreover, the Commandments point to some extent, by implication, to what the practice of a life of obedience will look like. They have thus had a tremendous influence on the concrete form and positive content of both the Jewish and the Christian life.

But when the Bible refers to the Law the reference is usually to that larger body of commandments found in the books of Genesis to Deuteronomy. It is now realized that that body of law grew over many centuries, and its growth can to some extent be traced. The discovery that the law 'of Moses' was, in fact, the outcome of a long process contradicts the notion that God's law is unchangeable. That is in itself of great significance. For it reminds us that obedience to God's will can never take place in a vacuum but always in the concrete situation in which people find themselves. Thus it is obvious that the provisions of Exodus 21: 7-11 no longer apply in a society where an unmarried woman can earn her keep in other ways than the only one open to her in antiquity. Similarly the instructions of Deuteronomy 23: 12-13 have become obsolete with proper plumbing.

But not only that. If it is true that God takes men where he finds them and guides them on from there, it is obvious that such guidance is done step by step. Thus the law is always relative to the actual conditions, not only the outward conditions but also the condition of the man who is expected to carry out the commandments. The obedience to God's will in the actual situation will create a new situation and new conditions, and then we shall be shown the next step. Incalculable harm can be done, and has in fact been done, by the imposition of what was quite honestly regarded as God's absolute demand but was not geared to the actual situation.

An obvious example is the demand made by some missionaries, working in societies with a polygamous tradition, that new converts should get rid of their surplus wives. It is, of course, one thing to teach that converts, after they have joined the Church, should not marry other wives if they already have one. It is quite a different thing to demand that men should cast out some of the wives they already have. But nobody seemed to think of the actual conditions or to be concerned about the plight of the dismissed women. The Bible does not make that kind of mistake (compare 1 Timothy 3: 2, 12: the demand that office-bearers must have only one wife seems to imply that there were members of the Church who had more than one).

But the opposite is also true. The *lex talionis* (Exodus 21: 12-27) makes an end of unlimited revenge and provides that punishment must not exceed the crime. It prevents a man being hanged for stealing a sheep or a boy having his hand cut off for pinching an apple. It is therefore one step on the road to a society where penalties for an offence are reduced to a minimum. It is absurd to quote it as an argument against the abolition of the death penalty, and we have Christ's authority for that (Matthew 5: 38-42). Similarly, the fact that slavery was not abolished, either by the Old Testament Law or by any of the New Testament authors, should never have been used as an excuse for the slave trade. Actually the slave trade is prohibited by the eighth commandment (Exodus 20: 15, which is not confined to the stealing of property but refers also, perhaps even specifically, to the stealing of people[7]). But so much effort is spent in the Law on the protection of slaves, and so much is done to alleviate the burdens and limit the extent of slavery (Deuteronomy 5: 12-15; 15: 12-18) that the next steps should have been obvious to anyone who really wished to know and do God's will.

The Law therefore needs a certain flexibility and is naturally subject to change in relation to new conditions and a new understanding of God's will. And it was, in fact, subject to such change until it became holy writ and thereby petrified.

But even so, the Law, any law, can only provide main outlines. It can never determine life from step to step. It can provide general directions but it can never deal with every possible case. Casuistry is an attempt to provide an answer to the questions which arise in every possible situation one might encounter. Such attempts one finds in Pharisaism and later Talmudic Judaism, in Roman Catholic moral theology, and also in various Protestant efforts. Casuistry is a noble attempt to put the whole of human life in all its variety under the direction of God's Law and to subject our behaviour entirely to God's will.

But it fails to produce true obedience because it abstracts the will of God both from the changing actual conditions and from the living God himself. It is simply not true that God wants all people always to do exactly the same things. There are certain things which one particular person has to do and which no one else can do for him. And there is a *kairos*, a specific appointed time when something has to be done that cannot be done at any other time: if one acts too soon the time is not yet ripe, if one hesitates and acts too late the opportunity to render obedience is gone. We have already indicated how Christ in his life rendered obedience to God in this precise sense, how he knew what God wanted him to do at the particular moment and acted accordingly (see pages 127-31).

That seems to qualify the validity of the Law, but it is in fact a recognition that the will of God concerns the whole of our lives and that obedience is something far more radical than the carrying out of certain commandments.[8] One is reminded of the boy whose parents had gone away for a few days, leaving him with the house and a host of instructions. However they had forgotten to say anything about the boat, and as 'all that is not forbidden is allowed', he takes it out to sea with a friend.[9] The adventures which are the result are no concern of ours, but the attitude, 'all that is not forbidden is allowed', is typical of a widespread kind of obedience that is not really obedience at all. Even if we do not quite sink to the level where we are for ever trying to find out how little will just do and how much we can get away with, it still holds good that if we do our duty we are unprofitable servants (Luke 17: 10).

Taking the situation into account, serving the *kairos* (Romans 12: 11),[10] is sometimes referred to as 'situation ethics'. There is no objection to the term so long as we remember that what should ultimately determine our action is not the situation but the Lord. That is what makes it obedience.

The obedience which Christ demands is no longer a formal obedience to a code of law, a commandment, or a general principle, but concrete obedience to a living Lord. His will is made known in a concrete situation. And there is no part of human life which is outside his dominion. Neither are there any actions which are neither commanded nor forbidden but only allowed; there is no neutral territory over which he has no command. Every act is either good or bad, there is no third possibility (compare Mark 3: 4).[11] That does not mean that in God's family there is no room for play: but such play is not indifferent but good because God-willed.

However, the will of God is not haphazard or inconsistent. God is love (see pages 105-10), and doing his will is an act of love, love of him who loves us and love of the others whom he loves.

Love, as understood by Christ (Mark 12: 29-33; Luke 10: 25-28), is not to be interpreted in a purely emotional sense. It is possible for us to wallow in feelings for others without ever getting into action. And we are certainly not required to like everybody. Our Lord knows the world in which we live and the kind of people we are likely to meet. He knows that there are many people about who are not at all likeable,

and that we all have our enemies. Loving our neighbour,
even the person we do not like, and even our enemy (Matthew 5: 44ff.) like ourselves, is a matter of accepting him
as he is, of having a real concern for him, of seeing his real
needs and doing whatever is required for his real interests.

That also implies standing where he stands, just as the
Lord Jesus Christ stood where we stand. Much Christian
charity falls short of the will of God because it is administered
from a distance. We are often prepared to go a long way to
meet our neighbour, even to meet him half-way or even
further. But there are limits beyond which most of us are
not prepared, indeed not able, to go. Our hesitation may
even have the best of reasons. Is there not the danger, if we
move too far away from our own place, especially if we move
out too far into a world of unbelief, vice and sin, that we ourselves may lose our way and even our faith? One cannot deal
with muck without getting dirty; one cannot identify oneself
with the world without becoming tainted. Is it not wiser to
lead circumspect lives?[12]

That danger is indeed not illusory, and warnings to that
effect are to be found in the New Testament (for example,
James 1: 27). But the aim of the Christian life is not to make
oneself good but to render obedience to Christ. If that
obedience demands that we should run the risk of getting
our hands dirty, then the risk must be taken. Ultimately the
responsibility for our sanctification is Christ's not ours. The
'perfection' demanded of us (Matthew 5: 48) is not moral
perfection but rather wholeness, being all of one piece, un-
divided, wholly on the Lord's side and at his disposal.[13] It
can be compared with the sense in which Dutch people
during the Nazi occupation used the word 'good'. A good
person was one who was wholly reliable in being on the
right side, who could be trusted to oppose the Nazis, who
was hungry and thirsty for righteousness. The word did not
refer to any of the more traditional moral qualities. It only
answered the question, 'Which side is he on?' Similarly, the
man who is perfect in the sense of the Bible is he who is

wholly on God's side. It has nothing to do with goodness as understood by philosophical ethics, let alone with human perfection. Such wholeness does not exclude, but on the contrary implies, a particular way of conduct, but conduct that consists in obedience at any risk, even the risk of getting ourselves morally or spiritually soiled.

The 'perfection' of Matthew 5: 48 is related to that righteousness which plays such a prominent part in both the Old and the New Testaments. It may seem surprising at first sight that so many people in the Old Testament regard themselves as righteous. It would, however, be a mistake to see that as a presumptuous valuation of their own moral perfection. They are righteous who take their proper place in the community that lives in the right relationship with God, the community that abides by his covenant and carries out his will. That implies a certain kind of conduct—for the carrying out of God's will is a practical matter on the level of ordinary secular existence—but in the final resort it is something that God gives, not something that man can achieve for himself.[14]

There is a way in which Christian obedience is 'other-worldly', not in the sense of an escape from the present world with its relationships and demands, but in that a Christian's allegiance is to the kingdom of God. His citizenship is 'in heaven' (Philippians 3: 20), but he is a soldier of Christ fighting on earth, not against flesh and blood, not against people, but against that power of evil that resists the will of his King. His standards are therefore not those of this world, however respectable, however high-minded, however religious, but his aims have the world in view, the world of people.

Obedience to Christ is rendered by the Church as a body, the body of Christ, the *laos*, the people of God, the laity. Within the context of that obedience the function of the ordained ministry is strictly one of service. This is not the place to deal with the significance and function of ordination, with the particular questions connected with the unique apostolic authority of the ministry of the word, with the problems surrounding the historical episcopate, and so on. Those problems and questions are indeed connected with the resurrection of our Lord, and they are of the greatest importance.[15] However, we are now concerned with other questions.

The ordained ministry has a vital and responsible part to play in the Church. But the widespread view of the Church as identical with the clergy or the ministers is a mistaken one, and one that can have serious consequences. The ministry is there to serve. It has been likened to the cook-house in the army.[16] That has an important job to do; but, though an army marches on its stomach, the cook-house is not an end in itself, nor is the real work of the army done in the mess.

The ministry covers a number of essential services in the Church. Some of those require certain abilities and skills, some special gifts, but also a considerable amount of knowledge and therefore a thorough training. For that reason it is sensible to keep a number of people employed full-time on those services. That does not mean that there is no room for a part-time ministry. Actually there is no intrinsic connexion between ordination and full-time employment in the Church. In Reformed and Presbyterian Churches elders are ordained to their office but they remain in their secular jobs. Most Churches would maintain that a priest or a minister who takes up other employment remains an ordained man. But it would be wasteful to use the fruits of an extensive and expensive training only part-time. Their full-time employment on a specific task in the Church, however, does not mean that they alone are full-time Christians. The laity are not part-time Christians. They are the Church, and the ministry is only a service, or rather, a number of services, within the Church and for the Church.

If the ministry is a service in the Church to the Church, then it is a service to the laity. The work of the minister is done to benefit the laity. That does not only mean that he is there to comfort them in their sorrows, help them in their troubles and guide them in their perplexities. That too, of course. But that would still be true if the laity were not the Church, and indeed every Christian minister will render those services to all and sundry, no matter whether they do or do not belong to the Church. The specific tasks of the minister in and for the Church are those which help its members to know the will of God and show and teach them how to carry it out and to be the Church in the world.

Many people seem to believe that whenever they avail themselves of those services, it should please and benefit the minister. Indeed, people often attend church services, Bible-study groups, training sessions, and so on, to please the minister. Naturally it will please any minister if people are eager to use his services. But it cannot possibly benefit him. Moreover, using his services to please him is as stupid as eating vegetables to please the greengrocer. The Church does not exist for the benefit of the ministers. Training a man for a job, paying him, perhaps not as much as would befit his training but certainly much more than most Churches can afford, and then not using his services is quite absurd.

If the laity are the Church, then the proclamation of the gospel to those who have not yet heard it is their job.[17] The minister may be the accredited ambassador of Christ, but the layman's task is not less important. Not only is he immune from the suspicion that he speaks about Christ only because it is his bread and butter (few people realize that the full-time ministry entails very real financial sacrifices). He is also more suited because he not only stands where others stand, but is seen to stand where they stand. Two things must however be stressed. The proclamation of the gospel, the presentation of God's love in Christ, is not only a matter of words. And presenting Christ to the world is not mere propaganda to further the interests of the Church: it is showing forth the truth, no matter what the results may be.

However, as we saw, the proper obedience to Christ is not

confined to the proclamation of the gospel. It is noteworthy that Christ's life for others was a life of *service without any strings attached*. He did not usually preach to the people whom he had cured from a disease or whom he had helped or served in any other way. Nor was it his custom to call them to follow him. Some did indeed follow him. But those whom he actually called had not first been conditioned by acts of healing or by other help. That is not to say that his preaching and healing were unrelated. They were both acts of obedience, and they both proclaim God's sovereign rule and his power to make men whole. In both his preaching and his healing people were confronted with the saving power of God. But Christ never used the service he rendered to people as a means to pressurize them into believing the gospel and following him. The gospel can only be received in perfect freedom (see page 75). Today the same still holds good. Christian action should never be a bait. It should be a matter of simple obedience, a work of love.

That the laity are the Church and that all are full-time Christians does not only mean that they should take their full share of the Church's work. It particularly does not only mean that the laity should be more active in 'religious' activities. To be sure, they should do that too, but there is more to it. A physician attending to his patients, a mother looking after her children, a dustman collecting refuse, a politician trying to solve the nation's problems, a teacher preparing a new generation for the future, they are all called to the same obedience to Christ, full-time obedience, in their own particular job. Doing voluntary work in one's spare time, doing the will of God in all those various activities which bring some light into other people's lives and are largely carried out by voluntary labour, is certainly an important part of Christian obedience. But it can never be our whole life, and our whole life should be obedience to God.

Those who are engaged in the more monotonous, unrewarding or even soul-destroying jobs will find it much harder to see their duty as God's will[18] and to render obedience to Christ in their daily work. But Ruth gleaning ears behind the reapers (Ruth 2: 3[19]) was carrying out God's will as much as the priests officiating in the Temple, and God is still the same. The preaching of the gospel, the healing of the sick, the cooking of meals, the education of the young, the building of our houses, the cleaning of our streets, they are all jobs that have to be done in God's world, and someone has to do them. One does not have to believe all kinds of romantic nonsense about the nobility of labour to see that. There are many kinds of labour which are not at all noble; some are downright degrading, and only a fool would enjoy doing them. Nevertheless, if they are necessary they have to be done, and someone has to do them.

That does not mean that every job is necessarily God's will. There are no doubt activities which serve neither God nor men nor the community. In choosing a career or a particular job a Christian, if he is serious about God's will, must ask himself if this is what God wants him to do. The question is a dangerous one, inasmuch as religious and utilitarian prejudices may well be mistaken for God's will. God is not interested in religion but in people, and a career 'in the Church', as a clergyman or a minister, is not necessarily more in accordance with his will than a secular career. Nor were the Puritans right in thinking that one could serve God only in useful jobs. God is no slave-driver but a father, and one can serve him also by entertaining people. Taking that into account, it remains important that one should ask, 'What does God want me to do?'

Christian obedience is not confined to the private sector. In the Old Testament God demands a just society. We have seen that it is only incidental that the New Testament does not say much about the subject (page 145). There is no doubt that the just society was never far from our Lord's mind (see, for example, Mark 12: 40; Matthew 5: 3-10; 23: 23-26;

Luke 4: 18-19; 6: 20-21). Luke, in fact, connects the coming of Christ specifically with that just society (Luke 1: 46-55).

One of the tragedies of the history of the Church is that its triumph in the Roman Empire was achieved from the top and used to support the tottering political fabric. We need not doubt Constantine's sincerity to observe that he lacked a vision of the political and social implications of the gospel.

The first attempt at the creation of a just society based on the gospel was made by Calvin at Geneva, in the sixteenth century. The base was too narrow, the will of God was often interpreted in a manner which we now find totally incomprehensible, and the attempt was short-lived. From a distance of four centuries it is easy for us to criticize the attempt and even to call it a tyranny (overlooking that the laws were devised by proper procedure, and that Calvin himself obeyed them even if he did not like them). But it was here that it was first understood that secular rulers ought to carry out the will of Christ in their own province. It was here that, in spite of the continuing social distinctions, all citizens were first regarded as equal before the law. It was here that the first attempt was made at a policy of price-control in order to protect the economically weak. It is easy to see that Calvin was no Amos, that there was too much restrictive religious legislation and too little social reform, but the problem and the task were at least seen, long before anyone else in authority saw them.

That it is the task of the secular authorities to do the will of Christ, to render obedience to Christ in their own province, does not mean that the State should do the work of the Church for her. Nor does it mean that one should aim at getting as many Christians in Parliament and eventually in the government as possible. The tasks of office are specific and are quite different from those of the Church. There is no reason to assume *a priori* that Christians will govern better, and more according to the will of Christ, than, say, humanists. Experience with non-Christian people in places of authority has not been encouraging, but neither has that

with Christian rulers in the past. What we are here concerned with is the task of the Church and the individual
Christian. That task is that they should demand a just
society and work towards it. And if Christians do find themselves in office, they should use their position, within its
given opportunities and limitations, to bring about that
society. For this is God's demand, not a country dominated
by priests or by the Church or by organized groups of
Christians, but a just society.

That demand will inevitably have to be worked out in
practical solutions for specific problems, and in our complex
modern world Christians will often differ on those solutions.
Moreover, it is unlikely that God's demand will coincide
with any particular party programme. There are severe
limitations to what Christians can do, even if they do find
themselves in positions of responsibility and authority. God's
demand remains: he demands, not that we should achieve
the impossible, but that we should render obedience to him.
A soldier cannot be held responsible if a battle is lost but he
is held responsible if he does not carry out orders.

The Church is entrusted with the gospel of the kingdom of
God. That implies that, through her authorized organs,
through her members, both as a group and as individuals,
and through specially commissioned bodies detailed to carry
out specific tasks, she has a number of things to do.

She has to proclaim the gospel of the Kingdom. That is to
say, she has to make known to the world that Jesus Christ is
the Lord. That mission of the Church is not particularly
popular, but that must not detract from the fact that it is
part of her commission, indeed the first part of her commission. She does not have to save souls, let alone save the
world. That has already been done. It is her task to tell and
show the world that it is God's world, and that it has been
saved.

She has to serve the real needs of people. As long as there
are real needs to be met—and we cannot yet foresee a future

in which that will no longer be the case—it is the task of the Church to do something about those needs.

She has to accompany the nation and the world with her prophetic criticism. The just society which God demands is always in the future.[20] The Church is therefore a protesting society. If she gets hurt in the process she should be neither surprised nor indignant. Her criticism should be positive and constructive. But she must never allow herself to become conformed to this world (Romans 12: 2), that is, to the past.[21]

And in all that she does she has to be really involved, as Christ himself was and is involved in the life of the world. Only so can her work be relevant and only so can it be obedience to her living Lord.

One fault of the Church as well as of individual Christians has often been that Christian obedience tended to degenerate into obedience to the supposedly unalterable commandments of a dead master, instead of the commands of a living Lord. It is not surprising that what Jesus wanted his disciples to do two thousand years ago is often totally irrelevant to the conditions of the twentieth century. We need the same courage as Paul and John, who did not always confine themselves to what Jesus said when he was in the flesh but tried to find out what he had to say to them and what he wanted of them in their own days, in their own circumstances. After all, he is not a dead master but a living Lord, and the Church ought to live by that. Thus we should ask what our living Lord, who was raised from the dead and is alive now, has to say to us today and what he wants us to do today and tomorrow. The Bible cannot give us a blueprint of Christian obedience in the twentieth century. Used properly it can help us to meet the living Christ and find out God's will for today.

God's will in Christ, though specific, is not haphazard. The risen Lord is the same as the Christ who lived in the flesh, and what he wants today is consistent with what he wanted for people and of people then—but that consistency, the unity of then and now, is a living, working unity.

The Christian life is not all work. Nor is Christian obedience a new slavery. The service of God is perfect freedom. That freedom becomes particularly active and fruitful in the manner in which a Christian can make his decisions and act on them. Once we have made a decision before God's face, knowing that God is with us, and taking into account God's will as we understand it, we can act without fear or worry. Like everyone else, we know that we can err, that we may have taken the wrong decision, that perhaps we have even misunderstood God's will. But we also know that we can leave the outcome to God.[22] The reconciliation with God in Christ, the forgiveness of our sins, is not an excuse for escaping the world and its responsibilities. But it does make us God's allies in facing those responsibilities, and thus gives our lives and work motivation, purpose and direction.

If that leaves us still heavy with the burden of our task and our responsibility, we ought to remind ourselves that the message of the resurrection is precisely not that we have to do this, that and the other, but that God is mighty and victorious, and that we are not alone in the world. The prevailing note is one of joy. Joy in God's love in Christ. Joy in our Christian fellowship. Joy in our hope. Joy also in our task. It can be fun to be a Christian, even though it is not always easy.

7. JESUS CHRIST: GOD'S PROMISE—OUR HOPE

We have so far not said much of the general resurrection of the dead, which is an inalienable aspect of the New Testament message of the resurrection of Christ. In the New Testament the resurrection of Christ is spoken of with his people in view, not only in the sense that he is returned to them and continues to be with them, but also in that his resurrection is inextricably tied up with theirs. Thus Paul makes it clear (1 Corinthians 15: 14ff.) that a denial of the general resurrection of the dead would make nonsense of the resurrection of Christ.[1] If there is no resurrection of the dead, then Christ was not raised. But, conversely, a denial of the resurrection of Christ would make nonsense of all Christian hope.[2]

The New Testament is extremely reticent about the life of the resurrection. Man has been given this earthly life, his present life: that is the only life he has. The eternal things are in the hands of God. But those eternal things include the resurrection of the dead.

The word is resurrection, not survival or immortality. We have already seen (pages 67-72) that the notion of any human immortality is foreign to the Bible. Though it has been a comfort to many people, it is actually a most uncomfortable notion. Imagine a whole eternity of being what we are now, only robbed of a body. Or, if we lack the necessary understanding of what we ourselves are, imagine a whole eternity of being surrounded by people as they are at present. Survival or immortality would mean continuation, continuation, that is to say, of our present trends. And the great majority of people do not improve as they get older. Not only do our bodies deteriorate—most theories of immortality dispense with those—but the mind becomes less alert, we become more entrenched in our prejudices, we also become more self-centred, more selfish and less kind. In fact, the mental, spiritual and moral deterioration that comes with old age is often much more distressing than that of the body. An endless continuation of the 'soul' with its sin and its natural aptitude for deterioration would, indeed, be the most distressing prospect imaginable. Resurrection, on the other hand, implies change (1 Corinthians 15: 51), renewal, indeed, a new creation.

It would be a mistake to equate the message of the resurrection with the sometimes rather massive forms in which the New Testament writers express it. Those forms are part of the language of the world in which they lived and to which they themselves belonged. They presuppose an understanding of the world which can no longer be ours. However, it was theirs. The New Testament writers had no other understanding of the world and no other terms in which to express themselves. It would be foolish to reject the gift of God because it has arrived in an old-fashioned package.

The word resurrection, as opposed to immortality, is not an abstract noun but a derivation from an active verb. Resurrection is an act of God. The hope of the resurrection is based, not on what we think of man, but on what we expect of God. It is not a piece of anthropology but belongs to the doctrine of God. And the doctrine of God, as we have seen (pages 105-26), is concerned with knowing him in action.

The message of the resurrection envisages a complete and full life. It does not regard the present life as something unworthy of the 'immortal soul', or the body as a prison from which the true self must be released. It affirms that the present life, in the secular world, in which we can be complete human beings, is God-given and good, and it will not believe that the life to come is going to be any less real or any less complete. It is very well aware that the present life is subject to the bondage of sin but it refuses to regard sin as inherent in the body that God has made. The Church does not speak of the resurrection because she wants to propagate a certain mythology (though it is difficult to speak of the resurrection other than in mythological terms). She has to speak of the resurrection of the dead because only thus can she maintain that the glory of the life to come will be no less concrete and no less real than that of the present life.

An important passage for the New Testament understanding of the resurrection of the dead is Mark 12: 24-27.[3] Here Jesus answers an objection made to the belief in the resurrection. The objection is based on contemporary popular views. Therefore, after the introductory verse 24, Jesus first corrects those views. The point of verse 25 is that the life of the resurrection is not a mere continuation of the old. The

conditions of the present life will no longer be in force. It is
not suggested that the raised dead will be disembodied
spirits (angels were not regarded as such).[4] All that Jesus
wants to say is that conditions will be different and that
marriage in its present form will no longer exist. No criticism
of sex is implied, but sex and marriage belong to the God-
given order of this life, and it would be absurd to project
them into the life of the resurrection.

That disposes of the objection but does not really support
the resurrection. It merely leaves the question open. It therefore seems unwarranted to delete the remainder of the
passage, as some interpreters suggest.[5] Verses 26-27 contain
the actual answer to the question of the resurrection. We
must not allow ourselves to be put off by the rabbinic form
of the argument. 'God said . . . "I am the God of Abraham,
and the God of Isaac, and the God of Jacob".' God 'is not
God of the dead, but of the living'. Therefore Abraham,
Isaac and Jacob must have been alive when those words
were spoken.[6] Surely that is not what the author meant?
No—but is it all that Jesus meant? That God is a God of
the living is a statement about God, not about the patriarchs.
It says something about what kind of a God he is. The hope
of the resurrection is based on the power and faithfulness of
God. It is a matter of knowing and trusting him. It is the
exact opposite of all those attempts ancient and modern to
prove that the dead are still alive. It has nothing to do with
necromancy, spiritualism or any doctrine of the soul. It is
not, nor can it be, based on any kind of anthropology. It
belongs entirely to the doctrine of God.

The belief in the resurrection of the body is therefore not
an attempt to look behind the curtain of death. It does not
deny, on the contrary, it confirms, that death is a barrier
beyond which we cannot spy. It affirms, with great emphasis, that from where we are death is the end. The eternal
things are in the hands of God. But, knowing him, we can be
quite confident. He is faithful and will not leave us. He raised
Jesus Christ from the dead and is able and willing to take

care both of our loved ones and of ourselves. Death is the end to us but not to him. This is the paradox of the Christian hope: after our end he will still be with us.

Resurrection of the dead is an eschatological notion. It speaks of the *eschaton*, not only of the individual but also and foremost of history and the world. There is therefore an inevitable tension between the assurance that the dead are in the hands of God now, and the expectation of the resurrection 'in the latter days'.

There have been various attempts to reconcile the two. Among those current in New Testament times one deserves mention because it has influenced the form of some New Testament sayings. Whereas it was taken for granted in most of the Old Testament that the dead are in Sheol, the realm of the dead (where they are really dead, whatever that may mean), it was later believed that the dead were awaiting the resurrection and the Last Judgment. That was, indeed, not the belief of all, but it was believed by many. During that time of waiting, Sheol would be the obvious place for them. But it was widely believed that there was some kind of distinction. The wicked were believed to be in Sheol (Hades in the New Testament; older translations render it as 'hell'), where they were kept in custody, awaiting the judgment; the righteous were not confined to Hades, they were, so to speak, 'let out on bail': they were in Paradise, waiting for the resurrection. As neither were properly alive we might think of their condition as a kind of sleep, with either pleasant or unpleasant dreams. Those views were by no means universal, but their influence is visible on the fringe of the New Testament.[7] Their form is, of necessity, mythological. Our conclusion must therefore stand, that the dead are in the hands of God, but that we know nothing beyond that. We are given the present life and are not meant to look beyond death. It is enough to know that beyond death we shall find Jesus Christ.

In spite of their mythological presentation, however, those

views remind us that there is an *eschaton* that is not yet. Though in the resurrection of Christ the *eschaton* has been revealed, there is a sense in which it is still coming. Its full consummation is still before us.

That full consummation is referred to as the Parousia of Christ. The term is usually interpreted as the 'return', the 'second coming' of Jesus Christ. Actually it just means his 'coming', his 'advent', and the word could be used legitimately of his incarnation. If, therefore, we want to speak of his 'second coming', we ought to remember that the 'second' is not in the original Greek and might indeed be an attempt to avoid certain awkward questions.

It is inevitable that any reference in the New Testament to the Parousia should be mythological in form. No one is capable of describing an event in other than historical terms, and any attempt to describe the *eschaton*, the event to end all history which is itself non-historical, in historical terms must be mythological in form. From the New Testament to Shane Leslie's 'Fleet Street'[8] it has been the one form in which we could express the expectation of the coming God, not adequately, but still better than in any other way.

Myth is an excellent, extremely attractive and very effective means of communication. But it would be absurd to confound it with history, and to look upon the presentation of the eschatological expectation in this form as a world history of the future. Within the context of human history the Parousia, the coming of God in Christ, will always remain future.[9] Yet the expectation of his coming is a real one.

But has God not come in Christ? Is he not with us in the risen Lord? Certainly. The incarnation was indeed a coming of God in history: a coming in the human condition, in the human flesh, in the man Jesus of Nazareth who was crucified under Pontius Pilate. Even so, that coming of God in Christ was not itself an event in history in the ordinary sense of the word. It was not something that can be examined by the methods of historical research. We can be reasonably certain, historically speaking, that there was a man Jesus, and consequently that he was born; but that God came in the flesh can only be grasped by faith. That Jesus died on the cross can be examined by historical methods, but that he died for us, and that in him God took our burdens upon himself, can be known only through faith. We can examine the case for and against the empty tomb, but whatever we find out will not bring us one step nearer to the certain knowledge, through faith, that Jesus Christ was raised from the dead.

Nevertheless we do believe that the Son of God was made man and came in the flesh, that he lived among us and died for our sins, that he was raised from the dead and is with us all the days until the end of time. And, if we do want to connect that with the eschatological expectation and the promise of his coming, his Parousia, then we can only do that within the context of a temporal, but that means a mythological, scheme. We shall never be able to dispense entirely with such temporal, mythological schemes as those of Korff and Cullmann.[10] We may, rightly, criticize them (see page 54), but we can never do without them. For we cannot escape, however much we try, from the categories of space and time by which all our thinking is governed.[11]

However, the scheme is not the content. The content of the Christian hope is Jesus Christ. The important question is not, 'What do we expect?' What really matters is whom we expect. We do not know what the future holds in store. Nobody knows *what* to expect. That holds good of the historical future; it holds good even more of the Parousia, the *eschaton*, the end of history. Describing the coming of Christ as a series of strange events, a cosmic catastrophe, may be useful as a means of communication, theologically it is a nonstarter. But we do know *whom* we expect: the same Jesus Christ who gave himself for us and whom we can trust, the risen Lord who overcame destiny and death. The Christian hope is not a matter of supernatural knowledge but of faith in a living Lord. We know whom we can trust for the present and the future and for eternity.

NOTES

INTRODUCTION

1. E.g. Walter Künneth, *The Theology of the Resurrection*, London, 1965; A. M. Ramsey, *The Resurrection of Christ*, London, 1945; G. W. H. Lampe and D. M. MacKinnon, *The Resurrection*, Oxford, 1966; C. F. D. Moule (ed.), *The Significance of the Message of the Resurrection for Faith in Jesus Christ*, London, 1968; C. F. Evans, *Resurrection and the New Testament*, London, 1970; Willi Marxsen, *The Resurrection of Jesus of Nazareth*, London, 1970; P. Benoit, *The Passion and Resurrection of Jesus Christ*, London, 1969.

2. Lampe and MacKinnon, *The Resurrection*, p.2.

3. Like the Sophists, many people today are more interested in whether a thing can be proved than whether it is true, conveniently forgetting that anything can be proved or disproved according to one's premises. It is only one step from sophistication to sophistry, the art of proving what one knows not to be true.

CHAPTER I

1. Mark's Narrative

1. Ernst Lohmeyer, *Das Evangelium des Markus* (Meyer), Göttingen, [16]1963, pp. 350-2; E. P. Gould, *The Gospel according to St Mark* (ICC), Edinburgh, 1895, p. 297.

2. Lohmeyer, *Markus*, p. 351.

3. Lampe and MacKinnon, *The Resurrection*, pp. 47-52; another view, Rudolf Bultmann, *The History of Synoptic Tradition*, Oxford, 1963, p. 290; Lohmeyer, *Markus*, p. 360.

4. J. van Goudoever in *Zoals er gezegd is over de Opstanding*, Hilversum/Antwerp, 1968, p. 39.

5. R. H. Lightfoot, *The Gospel Message of Mark*, Oxford, 1950, pp. 85ff.

6. Cf., e.g., C. E. B. Cranfield, *The Gospel according to St Mark*, Cambridge, 1959, p. 471.

7. Cf. B. H. Branscomb, *The Gospel of Mark* (Moffatt), London, 1937, p. 309.

8. Lohmeyer, *Markus*, p. 364.

9. Ibid., pp. 358-60; cf. also Lightfoot, *Gospel Message*, pp. 80-105; Sherman E. Johnson, *The Gospel according to St Mark* (Black), London, 1960, pp. 261-4. M. H. Bolkestein, *Het Verborgen Rijk*, (De Prediking van het NT), Nijkerk, 1954, p. 350, suggests that Mark intended to write a second volume.

10. Cf. Künneth, *Theol. Resurrection*, pp. 231ff.; Lohmeyer, *Markus*, p. 358.

11. Op. cit., p. 356.

2. Matthew's Narrative

1. Cf. Frank Morison, *Who Moved the Stone?*, London, 1930.

2. Kirsopp Lake, *The Historical Evidence for the Resurrection of Jesus Christ*, London, 1907, pp. 179-80.

3. Ernst Lohmeyer, *Das Evangelium des Matthäus* (Meyer, Sdb), Göttingen, [4]1967, p. 407, holds the opposite view.

4. The Trinitarian formula cannot have been used much before the end of the first century (if as early as that).

5. Cf. J. C. Fenton, *The Gospel of St Matthew* (Pelican), Harmondsworth, 1963, p. 452.

3. Luke's Narrative

1. Cf. G. B. Caird, *The Gospel of St Luke* (Pelican), Harmondsworth, 1963, p. 256.

2. A. R. C. Leaney, *The Gospel according to St Luke* (Black), London, 1958, pp. 28-31.

3. J. de Zwaan, *Inleiding tot het Nieuwe Testament*, Haarlem, 1941, I, p. 142; J. N. Sanders, *Those whom Jesus loved*, N. T. Studies, I, no. 1, 1954; Leaney, *Luke*, pp. 28ff.

4. Cf. Ernst Haenchen, *Die Apostelgeschichte* (Meyer), Göttingen, [10]1956, pp. 78-80, E. T. *The Acts of the Apostles*, Oxford, 1971.

5. Cf. Caird, *Luke*, p. 258.

6. Cf. ibid.

7. Cf. Emanuel Hirsch, *Die Auferstehungsgeschichten und der christliche Glaube*, Tübingen, 1940, p. 23.

4. The Narrative of the Acts

1. Haenchen, *Apgesch*, pp. 117-18; *pace* de Zwaan, *Inleiding*, I, p. 170, and many commentators.

2. Haenchen, loc. cit.

3. Gustav Stählin, *Die Apostelgeschichte* (NTD), Göttingen, [11]1966, p. 19, writes that the reading in codex D seems to suggest a vehicle; but that reading does not mean 'carried away', and a simple writer's error seems a much more likely explanation.

4. Cf. Stählin, loc. cit.

5. Haenchen, *Apgesch*, p. 122.

5. John's Narrative

1. Rudolf Bultmann, *Das Evangelium des Johannes* (Meyer), Göttingen, [14]1956, p. 527, E. T. *The Gospel of John*, Oxford, 1971, p. 680.

2. Ibid., p. 528 (E. T., p. 681).

3. Ibid.

4. Cf. Edwyn Hoskyns and F. N. Davey, *The Fourth Gospel*, London, [2]1947, p. 541; E. L. Smelik, *De Weg van het Woord* (De Prediking van het NT), Nijkerk, 1948, p. 282.

5. *Johannes*, p. 530 (E.T., p. 684).

6. Ibid.

7. Friedrich Spitta, *Das Johannesevangelium als Quelle der Geschichte Jesu*, 1910.

8. Cf. Bultmann, *Johannes*, p. 532 (E.T., p. 687).

9. Smelik, *De Weg van het Woord*, pp. 285-8, speaks of a 'Little Pentecost'.

10. Cf. J. H. Bernard, *The Gospel according to St John* (ICC), Edinburgh, 1928, II, p. 682.

11. Bultmann, *Johannes*, p. 539 (E.T., p. 696).

6. The Appearance by the Lakeside

1. William Manson, *The Gospel of Luke* (Moffatt), London, 1930, p. 48.

2. K. H. Rengstorf, *Das Evangelium nach Lukas* (NTD), Göttingen, [5]1949, p. 73; G. B. Caird, *Luke*, p. 91.

3. Since B. F. Westcott's commentary, *The Gospel according to St John*, London, 1908, there has been a persistent inclination to show the difference in translation (e.g. in J. B. Phillips's translation). The difference is still emphasized in Smelik's commentary (*De Weg van het Woord*, pp. 298-9) but most modern commentators rightly dismiss the idea of a deliberate distinction; cf. Hoskyns and Davey, *Fourth Gospel*, pp. 557-8; Bultmann, *Johannes*, p. 551 (E.T., p. 711); and especially Bernard, *John*, pp. 701-7.

7. Paul to the Corinthians

1. Ernst von Dobschütz, *Ostern und Pfingsten*, Leipzig, 1903.
2. Haenchen, *Apgesch*, pp. 227-84.
3. An excellent analysis in Hans Conzelmann, *Der erste Brief an die Korinther* (Meyer), Göttingen, 1969, pp. 296ff.
4. Cf. Karl Barth, *The Resurrection of the Dead*, London, 1933, p. 146; Jean Héring, *The First Epistle of Saint Paul to the Corinthians*, London, 1962, p. 160.

8. The Longer Ending of Mark

1. Lohmeyer, *Markus*, p. 364.
2. Bolkestein, *Het Verborgen Rijk*, p. 348. Cranfield, *Mark*, p. 472, speaks of a catechetical summary.
3. Cf. D. E. Nineham, *The Gospel of St Mark* (Pelican), Harmondsworth, 1963, p. 450.

9. Some Conclusions

1. The opposite view, Lohmeyer, *Markus*, p. 360; Bultmann, *Johannes*, p. 530 (E.T., p. 684).
2. F. C. Burkitt, *Christian Beginnings*, London, 1924, pp. 76-97.
3. Ibid., p. 88.
4. P. Gardner-Smith, *The Narratives of the Resurrection*, London, 1926, pp. 135ff.
5. Cf. Cranfield, *Mark*, p. 463, and other commentaries.
6. Gardner-Smith, *Narratives*, p. 144.
7. Consequently Paul's emphatic statement that the risen Lord appeared first to Peter has been deleted from the Gospels, Manson, *Luke*, p. 280.
8. But cf. Nineham, *Mark*, pp. 447f., for other suggestions.
9. R. Gregor Smith, *Secular Christianity*, London, 1966, p. 103.
10. Cf. Lampe and MacKinnon, *The Resurrection*, pp. 27-70.
11. Van Goudoever, in *Zoals er gezegd is over de Opstanding*, pp. 29-31.
12. This makes Lake's suggestions (*Evidence*, pp. 182ff.), though not impossible, totally irrelevant.
13. Willem de Merode, *Het Kostbaar Bloed*, Amsterdam, 1922, p. 59.

CHAPTER 2

1. The Resurrection of Christ and History

1. This is what makes the notion of *Heilsgeschichte*, 'saving history', so unsatisfactory. Some pertinent comments by Lampe, *The Resurrection*, pp. 32-3.

2. Since Kant's *Critique of Pure Reason* that can scarcely be questioned.

3. In spite of Lohmeyer's comments, *Markus*, p. 558.

4. H. J. Heering, *De Opstanding van Christus*, Amsterdam, 1946.

5. Karl Barth, *Die kirchliche Dogmatik*, I², Zollikon-Zürich, ³1945, pp. 50-76, E.T. *Church Dogmatics*, I², Edinburgh, 1956, pp. 45-70.

6. Rudolf Bultmann, *Theologie des neuen Testaments*, Tübingen, ³1958, p. 4, E.T. *Theology of the New Testament*, I, London, 1952, p. 5.

7. Bultmann, *Johannes*, p. 530 (E.T., p. 684).

8. Ibid.

9. But Spitta, *Johannesev. als Quelle*, solves the problem by deleting verse 8b, cf. p. 30.

10. Bultmann, *Johannes*, pp. 539-40 (E.T., p. 696).

11. Cf. Caird, *Luke*, pp. 258-9.

12. It is therefore not necessary to postulate different sources, cf. Haenchen, *Apgesch*, p. 282.

13. Barth, *Resurrection of the Dead*, p. 141.

14. Paul, in 1 Corinthians 15: 35-50, is not attempting to answer the question, how; the point of his argument is precisely that it cannot be answered (though it is indeed asked, cf. Conzelmann, *I Kor.*, p. 35).

15. F. W. A. Korff, *Christologie, de leer van het Komen Gods*, 2 vols., Nijkerk, 1940-41.

16. Oscar Cullman, *Christ and Time*, London, 1951.

17. Cf. Karl Barth, *KD*, I¹, pp. 40ff. (E.T., pp. 43ff.); for different approaches to related problems cf. Kornelis Heiko Miskotte, *When the Gods are Silent*, London, 1967; and Harvey Cox, *On Not Leaving it to the Snake*, London, 1968, pp. 3-13.

2. Resurrection and Eschatology

1. Albert Schweitzer, *The Mysticism of Paul the Apostle*, London, 1931, p. 98.

2. Ibid., p. 99.

3. Heering, *Opstanding*, p. 209.

4. Neither the expectation of the resurrection in the age to come, nor the beliefs about Enoch, Moses and Elijah, are true parallels.

5. Cf. Karl Barth, *Der Römerbrief*, Zollikon-Zürich, [8]1947, p. 484, E.T. *The Epistle to the Romans*, London, 1933, p. 500.

6. Cf. Wilhelm Vischer, *Das Christuszeugnis des alten Testaments*, II, Zollikon-Zürich, [2]1946, pp. 173-8, 197-201.

3. Resurrection and Myth

1. R. Reitzenstein, *Die hellenistischen Mysterienreligionen*, Leipzig, 1920.

2. W. Bousset, *Kyrios Christos*, Göttingen, 1913.

3. Karl Barth, *Römerbrief*, p. 6 (E.T., p. 30); but in *KD*, II[1], his views have changed considerably.

4. Emil Brunner, *Der Mittler*, Tübingen, [2]1930, pp. 337ff., E.T. *The Mediator*, London, 1934, pp. 377ff.

5. *Offenbarung und Heilsgeschehen*, Munich, 1941, and elsewhere.

6. Künneth, *Theol. Resurrection*, p. 48.

7. E. Unger, *Wirklichkeit, Mythus, Erkenntnis*, Berlin, 1931, p.164.

8. Künneth, *Theol. Resurrection*, p. 48.

9. Paul Tillich in *Die Religion in Geschichte und Gegenwart*, Tübingen, [2]1930, IV, col. 364, E.T., *Twentieth Century Theology in the Making*, London, 1970, II, p. 344.

10. A. Titius, *Ist systematische Theologie als Wissenschaft möglich?*, Berlin, 1931, p. 164.

11. G. van der Leeuw, *Phänomenologie der Religion*, Tübingen, 1933, p. 389; the E.T., *Religion in Essence and Manifestation*, London, 1938, p. 413, loses part of the point, as *Begehung* is not only 'celebration' but also 'perpetration', the 'carrying out'.

12. 'Of course, nobody believes in the Real Absence'; John Huxtable.

13. Cf. Bultmann, *Theol. N.T.*, p. 127 (E.T., I, p. 124).

14. P.-L. Couchoud, *Le Mystère de Jésus*, Paris, 1924, p. 108.

15. Ibid., p. 137.

16. Ibid., p. 90; Couchoud leans heavily on the work of Loisy, but the latter reaches entirely different conclusions; cf., e.g., Alfred Loisy, *Jésus et la tradition évangélique*, Paris, 1910.

17. *Kerygma und Mythus*, I, p. 177.

18. *Der Mittler*, p. 347 (E.T., p. 387).

19. Euripides, *Herakles*, 38; cf. G van der Leeuw, *Goden en menschen in Hellas*, Haarlem, 1927, p. 78.

4. Resurrection and Cosmology

1. John A. T. Robinson's picture in *Honest to God*, London, 1963, pp. 11ff., is a caricature but not entirely untrue.

2. Quoted by W. Elert, *The Structure of Lutheranism*, Saint Louis, 1962, p. 417; cf. Korff, *Christologie*, II, p. 283.

3. E. L. Mascall, *Christian Theology and Natural Science*, London, 1956.

4. Weimarer Ausgabe (Luther, *Werke*, *Kritische Gesamtausgabe*, ed. J. C. F. Knaake, Weimar, 1883-), 23, pp. 28-231; 26, pp. 251-509; cf. T. Harnack, *Luthers Theologie*, II, 1927, pp. 186ff., 219.

5. 'I did not need that hypothesis', referring to God, attributed to Pierre-Simon de Laplace.

5. Resurrection and Immortality

1. H. Denzinger and A. Schönmetzer, *Enchiridion symbolorum definitionum et declarationum*, Freiburg, [34]1967, no. 1440 (=738 in editions before 1963).

2. For example by B. Delfgaauw in *Zoals er gezegd is over de Schepping*, Zeist/Antwerp, 1962, p. 124.

3. Cf. W. A., 10.ii.2, pp. 117ff.

4. *Institutes of the Christian Religion*, I. xv. 2.

5. Johannes Wolleb, *Christianae theologiae compendium*, Basel, 1626, 29.

6. Peter van Mastricht, *Theoretico-practica theologia*, Utrecht/Amsterdam, [2]1725, III. ix. 17.

7. H. Bavinck, *Gereformeerde Dogmatiek*, Kampen, 1901, IV, p. 692.

8. G. van der Leeuw, *Onsterfelijkheid of Opstanding*, Assen, [4]1947; id., *La Religion dans son essence et ses manifestations*, Paris, 1955, pp. 330-1 (not in the English ed.).

9. *Theology of the Resurrection*.

10. *The Resurrection of the Dead*; also in *KD*.

11. *Gilgamesh*, Table 10.

12. For similar sentiments in Greece, cf. C. Kerenyi, *The Religion of the Greeks and Romans*, London, 1962, pp. 261ff.

13. Cf. Walther Eichrodt, *Theology of the Old Testament*, London, 1967, II, p. 497.

14. *Pace* W. O. E. Oesterley, *The Psalms*, London, ²1954, pp. 91, 354.

15. Matthew 10:28 is the exception.

16. If there were no other reasons, 1 Thessalonians 5:23 would almost suffice to raise doubts as regards the Pauline authorship of the Epistles to the Thessalonians.

17. But Revelation 16:3 should warn us not to press.

18. Cf. Korff, *Christologie*, II, p. 221; A. Oepke in Gerhard Kittel's *Theologisches Wörterbuch zum neuen Testament*, Stuttgart, 1933-, II, p. 334. Translations do not always distinguish clearly between 'rising' and 'being raised'.

6. Resurrection and Faith

1. G. van der Leeuw, *Inleiding tot de Phaenomenologie van den Godsdienst*, Haarlem, 1948, p. 140; cf. Calvin, *Institutes*, III. xxiv. 3.

2. Pascal speaks of a 'wager': Blaise Pascal, *Pensées*, ed. L. Brunschwicg, Paris, 1897, no. 233, ed. L. Lafuma, Paris, ²1953, E.T. by J. Warrington, London, 1960, no. 233.

3. St Bernard; also Pascal, *Pensées*, Brunschwicg, 553, Lafuma, 739.

4. Van der Leeuw, *Inleiding*, p. 140.

5. *êmunah*; the usual meaning is, 'faithfulness', 'fidelity'. Habakkuk 2:4 is the only place where it could possibly mean 'faith', but here too '[God's] faithfulness' seems preferable.

6. *pistis*; outside the New Testament it usually means 'faithfulness', but is sometimes used meaning 'faith'.

7. Cf. my paper, 'Paul's doctrine of justification and its Old Testament roots', to be published in *Studia Evangelica*, VI (T.U.), Berlin.

8. From *religare*, 'to bind', or from *relegere*, 'to observe carefully'.

9. Pascal, *Mémorial* (in the Bibliothèque Nationale in Paris, with the *Pensées* manuscript, *fr.*9202), Lafuma, 737; Jean-Paul Sartre, *Le diable et le bon dieu*, Paris, 1951; cf. J. J. Buskes, *God en mens als concurrenten*, Amsterdam, 1968, pp. 7-16.

10. Pascal, *Pensées*, Brunschwicg, 227, Lafuma, 224.

7. Conclusion

1. Barth, *Römerbrief*.

2. Cf. Giovanni Miegge, *Gospel and Myth in the Thought of Rudolf Bultmann*, London, 1960, p. 101.

CHAPTER 3

1. The Risen Lord Restores the Relationship

1. Though, according to the Gospels, others sometimes did.
2. T. F. Glasson, 'The Kingdom as Cosmic Catastrophe', *Studia Evangelica*, III (T.U. 88), Berlin, 1964, p. 187.
3. Bultmann, *Theol. N.T.*, p. 3 (E.T., p. 4).
4. Glasson, 'The Kingdom', p. 190.
5. K. L. Schmidt in Kittel, *Th. Wb.*, I, p. 586, E.T. *Basileia, Bible Key Words*, London, 1957, VII, p. 45.
6. Bultmann, *Theol. N.T.*, p. 5 (E.T., p. 6).
7. The translation, 'The kingdom of God is within you', is possible but unlikely; cf. Bultmann, *Theol. N.T.*, p. 5 (E.T., p. 6); Leaney, *Luke*, p. 230; Rengstorf, *Lukas*, pp. 194f.; Caird, *Luke*, p. 197; but also Hans Conzelmann, *An Outline of the Theology of the New Testament*, London, 1969, p. 112.
8. C. H. Dodd, *The Parables of the Kingdom*, London, 1936.
9. Cf. 1 Samuel 16:7, where one should surely translate, 'Man sees with his eyes but YHVH sees with his heart'; this is the only rendering that does justice to the parallelism of the Hebrew text; cf. Vischer, *Christuszeugnis*, II, p. 198.
10. Dietrich Bonhoeffer, *Letters and Papers from Prison*, enlarged ed., London, 1971, p. 382.
11. Martin Buber, *I and Thou*, New York, [2]1958.

2. God was in Christ

1. Korff, *Christologie*, II, pp. 226ff.
2. Bultmann, *Johannes*, p. 539 (E.T., p. 696).
3. Korff, *Christologie*, II, p. 235.
4. Barth, *KD*, I[2], p. 126 (E.T., p. 114).
5. Cf. Miskotte throughout his book, *When the Gods are Silent*.
6. W. Wrede, *Das Messiasgeheimnis in den Evangelien*, Göttingen, 1901.
7. G. Strecker, 'Zur Messiasgeheimnistheorie im Markusevangelium', in *Studia Evangelica*, III, p. 96.
8. Wrede, *Messiasgeheimnis*.
9. Robinson, *Honest to God*, p. 73.
10. Cf. Otto Michel, *Der Brief an die Römer* (Meyer), Göttingen, [12]1963, p. 38.
11. Ibid.
12. The question how much of Romans 1:3 is Paul's own and

how much is dependent on tradition is interesting, but irrelevant to our purpose.

13. C. H. Dodd, *The Epistle of Paul to the Romans* (Moffatt), London, 1932, p. 5.

14. G. Sevenster, *De Christologie van het Nieuwe Testament*, Amsterdam, 1946, pp. 148-9.

15. Cf. Bultmann, *Theol. N.T.*, pp. 130ff. (E.T., pp. 128ff.)

16. Sevenster, loc. sit.

17. YHVH (*Yahve* or *Yahu*), usually spoken *Adonai*, 'Lord'.

18. Bousset, *Kyrios Christos*, 1913; Bultmann, *Theol. N.T.*, p. 127 (E.T., p. 124).

19. *Christos*.

20. Linguistic evidence seems to exclude Paul. On the other hand the letter does not make sense unless written by Paul. Was it written, on his behalf, by one of his helpers?

21. Bultmann, *Theol. N.T.*, p. 178 (E.T., p. 175).

22. Leaney, *Luke*, pp. 20-8.

23. Ibid.

24. Bernard, *John*, pp. xciii-xciv.

25. Bultmann, *Johannes*, pp. 1-57 (E.T., pp. 13-83).

26. Sevenster, *Christologie*, p. 225; Eichrodt, *Theol. O.T.*, II, pp. 69ff.

27. Sevenster, loc. cit.; J. Pedersen, *Israel, its Life and Culture*, London, 1926, I, pp. 167ff.

28. Miskotte, *When the Gods are Silent*.

29. Cf. G. van Leeuwen, 'Kennis nemen van de radicale theologie noodzakelijk', *Hervormd Nederland*, The Hague, 2.9. 1967, p.4.

30. Bultmann, *Johannes*, p. 16 (E.T., p. 33).

31. Reconstruction by Hans Lietzmann, *Sitzungsbericht der Akademie der Wissenschaften*, Berlin, 1919. Similar forms, Denzinger, nos. 1-5 (=1). Cf. Oscar Cullmann, *Die ersten christlichen Glaubensbekenntnisse*, Zollikon-Zürich, 1943.

32. From a letter of Marcellus of Ancyra to Julian I of Rome, quoted by Epiphanius of Salamis, *Panaria* lxxii.3[1]; also E. Klostermann, *Die Fragmente Marcells*, Leipzig, 1906, no. 129; cf. Denzinger, no. 11 (=2).

33. The Council of Nicaea was only one stage in the development of the Trinitarian dogma; cf. Adolf von Harnack, *Lehrbuch der Dogmengeschichte*, Tübingen, [4]1909, II, pp. 184-284, E.T. *History of Dogma*, New York, 1961, IV, pp. 1-107. The Creed

R.R.—M

defined at Nicaea, Denzinger, no. 125 (=54); that defined at Constantinople (the so-called Nicene Creed), Denzinger, no. 150 (=86).

34. *homoousios.*

35. *homoiousios.*

36. Cf. Harnack, *History of Dogma*, IV, p. 223.

37. Cf. K. H. Miskotte, *De Kern van de Zaak*, Nijkerk, 1950, pp. 265ff.

38. Denzinger, no. 302 (=148).

39. Harnack, *History of Dogma*, IV, p. 223.

40. There was, of course, also a secular, and indeed, an antichristian side to eighteenth-nineteenth-century thought.

41. Cf. van Leeuwen's article in *Hervormd Nederland*, 2.9.1967.

42. William Hamilton and Thomas Altizer, *Radical Theology and the Death of God*, Indianapolis, 1966.

43. Dietrich Bonhoeffer, *Akt und Sein*, Munich, ²1956, p. 94, E.T. *Act and Being*, London, 1962, p. 126.

44. The frequently misquoted phrase does not mean, 'as if there was no God'.

45. K. H. Miskotte, *Kennis en Bevinding*, Haarlem, 1969, pp. 13-15.

46. Friedrich Nietzsche, *Die fröhliche Wissenschaft*, 1881, no. 125; cf. Miskotte, *Kennis en Bevinding*, pp. 214ff.

47. Cf. Buskes, *God en Mens als concurrenten*, pp. 49ff.

48. In spite of the title of the book referred to.

49. His cry on the cross, Mark 15:34, Matthew 27:46 (Matthew obviously corrects Mark; codex D may well contain the correct reading), is a quotation from Psalm 22. This psalm ends in hope. That, however, does not mean that the experience of God-forsakenness was any less real as an experience. On the contrary, it is characteristic of a number of laments in the Psalms (e.g. Psalms 31, 42-43, as well as 22) that the very real *experience* of the absence of God is overcome by the *knowledge*, through faith, of his presence.

3. *The Risen Christ: the Truth about God*

1. Cf. Karl Barth, *Credo*, London, 1936, pp. 95ff.

2. Cf. Nineham, *Mark*, p. 35.

3. Smelik, *De Weg van het Woord*, pp. 50ff.

4. Cf. Paul Winter, *On the Trial of Jesus* (Studia Judaica I), Berlin, 1961.

5. There is probably no significance in the variation of the words; see p. 34.

6. In the New Testament, and also later in the Church, the word 'grace' is variously used of God's unmerited favour towards man and of the effect of that favour on him, sometimes also in the plural of the gifts which God bestows on man. Thomas Aquinas speaks of uncreated and created grace. We are here concerned with the first.

7. *ḥēn.*

8. *gein* in the dialect of the Amsterdam Jews.

9. Conzelmann, *Outline*, p. 216; cf. George A. F. Knight, *A Christian Theology of the Old Testament*, London, 1959, pp. 245f.

10. Conzelmann, *Outline*, p. 240.

11. But *ṣᵉdaqa*, 'righteousness', is never used for retributive or punitive justice; cf. K. Koch, *SDQ im alten Testament*, diss., Heidelberg, 1953; Gerhard von Rad, *Old Testament Theology*, Edinburgh, 1962, p. 377.

12. Eichrodt, *Theol. O.T.*, I, p. 241; Conzelmann, *Outline*, p. 216.

13. Anselmus, *Cur Deus Homo?*, Migne, *Patrologia Latina*, 158-9.

14. Bultmann, *Theol. N.T.*, p. 287 (E.T., p. 287); F. Büchsel, *Theologie des neuen Testaments*, Gütersloh, 1935, pp. 100, 102, 180; Dodd, *Romans*, pp. 51-3; Paul Feine, *Theologie des neuen Testaments*, Leipzig, 1936, pp. 168, 310; Korff, *Christologie*, II, p. 188; J. de Zwaan, *Imperialisme van den Oudchristelijken Geest*, Haarlem, 1919, pp. 181ff.

15. H. Rashdall, *The Idea of the Atonement in Christian Theology*, London, 1925, p. 435.

16. Walter Schmithals in the *Siebenstern* reprint of Rudolf Bultmann, *Jesus*, Munich/Hamburg, [3]1967, p. 157.

17. Harnack, *History of Dogma*, VI, p. 77. For a thorough discussion, both of the merits of Anselm's theory and the objections to it, Harnack's work is unsurpassed.

18. Dodd, *Romans*, p. 52.

19. Barth, *Römerbrief*, p. 16 (E.T., p. 40).

20. '*Credo in deum patrem omnipotentem*'.

21. E.g., Job 5:17; but not Genesis 17:1.

22. E.g., Hosea 12:6; but not Isaiah 6:3.

23. The words 'says the LORD, the Pantokrator', are not in the passages cited (2 Samuel 7:14; Isaiah 43:6; Jeremiah 31:9) but

were evidently formed in analogy with the Hebrew text (not the LXX version) of Jeremiah 7:3, etc.

24. That the visions may have been a literary device does not affect the point.

25. There are many examples in mosaic in Byzantine churches. A famous panel painting is the top centre panel of Jan van Eyck's *Adoration of the Lamb* in Gent cathedral.

26. Reincarnation; *samsara* is generally regarded as a burden.

27. There are, indeed, slight traces of its terminology (e.g., Matthew 10:28) but these cannot be regarded as evidence that any New Testament author believed in the immortality of the soul.

28. Karl Barth, *A Shorter Commentary on Romans*, London, 1959, p. 21.

29. Most translators disregard the specific meaning of the phrase 'all the days', and render 'always'.

4. Jesus Christ: the Truth about Man

1. Barth, *Römerbrief*, p. 175 (E.T., p. 195); cf. *KD*, I², pp. 120-5 (E.T., pp. 109-13).

2. '*Non posse non peccare*', Augustine.

3. Cf. Conzelmann, *Outline*, pp. 195ff.; Bultmann, *Theol. N.T.*, pp. 251ff. (E.T., I, pp. 250ff.).

4. Bonhoeffer, *Letters and Papers*, p. 382.

5. Bultmann, *Jesus and the Word* (E.T. of *Jesus*), London, 1962, pp. 11ff.

6. Dorothy L. Sayers, *The Man Born to be King*, London, [16]1951, p. 121.

7. Winter, *On the Trial of Jesus*.

8. Jacobus Revius, *Over-ysselsche Sangen en Dichten*, Deventer, 1630, p. 315.

9. Brunner, *Der Mittler*, p. 3 (E.T., p. 21).

10. Conzelmann, *Outline*, p. 171.

11. Cf. Barth, *Römerbrief*, p. 407 (E.T., p. 421): the criterion of the double predestination is in the repeated *all* of chapter 11:32.

12. Cf. Conzelmann, *Outline*, pp. 171-3.

5. The Body of Christ

1. Cf. John A. T. Robinson, *The Body*, London, 1952, p. 49.

2. Ibid., p. 50.

3. Joachim Jeremias, *Die Abendmahlsworte Jesu*, Göttingen, 1935, pp. 86-94.

4. The discourse on the bread of life, John 6:26-58, cannot be divorced from the Eucharist.

5. E. Mersch, *The Whole Christ*, London, 1949, p. 104; Robinson, *The Body*, p. 58.

6. *rōsh.*

7. Cf. Barth *Römerbrief*, p. 428 (E.T., p. 443).

8. Speaking of the 'mystical body of Christ' is therefore not necessarily mistaken but tends to obscure the main point: what is at issue is not so much the nature of the Church but rather the will of Christ.

9. Cf. Barth, *A Shorter Commentary on Romans*, p. 162.

10. It is significant that the early Christian basilica was designed specifically as a banqueting hall for the celebration of the Eucharist; cf. F. van der Meer, *Oudchristelijke Kunst*, Zeist/Antwerp, 1959, pp. 51-69.

6. *Jesus Christ the Lord*

1. *didachē = doctrina*, cf. Matthew 28:20.

2. Hendrik Kraemer, *The Christian Message in a Non-Christian World*, London, 1938, p. 178.

3. Cf. Gerhard von Rad, *Das erste Buch Mose* (ATD), Göttingen, [3]1953, pp. 71-2, E.T., *Genesis*, London, 1961, pp. 86-7.

4. Sons of *Elohim*; translators will render 'sons of God', without taking into account that Genesis 6:1-4 is a Yahvist passage. This author does not normally call the God of Israel *Elohim*; he uses the word in the sense of supernatural beings other than YHVH; 'sons of gods' would be a much better translation.

5. The New Testament part of the New English Bible is particularly apt to introduce notions foreign to the original, e.g., 'unspiritual nature' (Romans 7:25), 'lower nature' (Romans 8:3), 'bodily appetites' (Romans 13:14); all suggest a dualism between body and soul or between a lower and a higher nature which the original *sarx*, 'flesh', does not contain. *Sarx* refers to the human condition, not to man's nature.

6. A. M. Brouwer, in his Dutch translation of the New Testament renders (correctly), 'First seek his kingly rule (*koningschap*) and the righteousness he demands', H. T. Obbink and A. M. Brouwer, *De Bijbel*, Amsterdam, 1927, III, p. 12.

7. Cf. Martin Noth, *Exodus*, London, 1962, pp. 165-6.

8. Bultmann, *Jesus and the Word*, pp. 58ff.

9. Manfred Hausmann, *Abel mit der Mundharmonika*, Frankfurt am Main, ⁷⁵1940.

10. In spite of the MS support for 'serve the Lord', we regard 'serve the *kairos* (the time, the opportune moment)' as the more likely reading. Cf. Michel, *Römer*, p. 304; also Barth, *Römerbrief*, pp. 435, 441 (E.T., pp. 450, 457); and Calvin's *Commentary on the Epistle to the Romans*.

11. Bultmann, *Jesus and the Word*, pp. 61f.

12. Cf., for instance, the ordination questions for ministers in the Presbyterian Church of England.

13. Cf. Julius Schniewind, *Das Evangelium nach Matthäus* (NTD), Göttingen, ⁸1956, p. 73.

14. Von Rad, *O.T. Theology*, pp. 370-83.

15. As the gospel is a message not only about but from the risen Christ, the heart of the matter is the question of the credentials of those who claim to be Christ's ambassadors.

16. Cox, *On Not Leaving it to the Snake*, p. 99.

17. J. C. Hoekendijk, *The Church Inside Out*, London, 1966, p. 121.

18. 'O God, who hast . . . set men in [Toc H] to see their duty as Thy will . . . ': the Toc H prayer.

19. K. H. Miskotte, *Het Gewone Leven*, Amsterdam, undated, pp. 140ff.

20. Cox, *On Not Leaving it to the Snake*, pp. 11-13.

21. Cf. Barth, *Römerbrief*, p. 419 (E.T., p. 434).

22. 'Sin boldly' (Luther). The expression is not meant to suggest that sin does not matter, but that we should not allow the fear of being mistaken and perhaps sinning to paralyse our ability to make decisions and to act.

7. *Jesus Christ: God's Promise—our Hope*

1. Barth, *Resurrection of the Dead*, p. 161.

2. Künneth, *Theol. Resurrection*, pp. 224-7; cf. D. H. van Daalen, 'The Resurrection of the Body and Justification by Grace', *Studia Evangelica*, III (T.U. 88), Berlin, 1964, p. 219.

3. Cf. D. H. van Daalen, 'Some Observations on Mark 12:24-27', *Studia Evangelica*, IV (T.U. 102), Berlin, 1968, pp. 241ff.

4. Bolkestein, *Het Verborgen Rijk*, p. 261.

5. Bultmann, *Syn. Trad.*, p. 26.

6. Cf. 4 Maccabees 7:19; 16:25. Similar arguments are attributed to R. Gamaliel and R. Jonathan (quoted Nineham, *Mark*, p. 321).

7. Of later attempts to reconcile the biblical references to those views with the Greek teaching of the immortality of the soul we mention the *Westminster Confession*, Ch. 32.

8. Padraic Colum, Shane Leslie and others, *Eyes of Truth*, London, 1910, p. 27.

9. Cf. Barth, *Römerbrief*, p. 484 (E.T., p. 500); some valuable insights are also found in Cox, *On Not Leaving it to the Snake*, pp. 11ff.

10. Korff, *Christologie*; Cullman, *Christ and Time*, cf. p. 54.

11. On this subject Kant's *Critique of Pure Reason* is still unsurpassed.

INDEX OF NAMES AND SUBJECTS

INDEX OF BIBLE REFERENCES